JESUS SAID, "I AM THE RESURRECTION
AND THE LIFE; HE WHO BELIEVES IN ME,
THOUGH HE DIE, YET SHALL HE LIVE,
AND WHOEVER LIVES AND BELIEVES IN ME
SHALL NEVER DIE."
JOHN 11:25

Also by J. Isamu Yamamoto:

Hare Krishna, Hare Krishna (booklet)
The Moon Doctrine (booklet)
The Puppet Master: An Inquiry into Sun Myung
    Moon and the Unification Church (book)

BEYOND BUDDHISM

A basic introduction to the Buddhist tradition

J. Isamu Yamamoto

INTER-VARSITY PRESS
DOWNERS GROVE
ILLINOIS 60515

InterVarsity Press is the book-publishing division of Inter-Varsity Christian Fellowship, a student movement active on campus at hundreds of universities, colleges and schools of nursing. For information about local and regional activities, write IVCF, 233 Langdon St., Madison, WI 53703.

Distributed in Canada through InterVarsity Press, 1875 Leslie St., Unit 10, Don Mills, Ontario M3B 2M5, Canada.

ISBN 0-87784-990-0

Printed in the United States of America

Library of Congress Cataloging in Publication Data

Yamamoto, J. Isamu.
    Beyond Buddhism.

    Bibliography: p.
    Includes index.
        1. Buddhism.   2. Christianity and other
religions–Buddhism.   3. Buddhism–Relations–
Christianity.   I. Title.
BQ4012.Y35   294.3   81-17180
ISBN 0-87784-990-0   AACR2

17	16	15	14	13	12	11	10	9	8	7	6	5	4	3	2	1
95	94	93	92	91	90	89	88	87	86	85	84	83	82			

TO RON

PREFACE

When I was in Tokyo, I had an interesting discussion with a Japanese friend. His parents are devout Nichiren Buddhists but he is the director of KGK, a thriving Christian outreach to students. I mentioned that Americans, particularly Christian Americans, do not understand Buddhism. I said that many of them assume that the Buddha was a Japanese. He laughed and replied, "It seems that Americans and Japanese do not know each other's religions very well. Many Japanese think that Jesus was an American."

How unfortunate that cultural presumptions cloud our comprehension of the beliefs of other people! This book endeavors to cut through the clouds and present a clearer view of Buddhism. This is a brief overview of the history and the philosophies of Buddhism, not a scholarly study of any one school of Buddhism. It is not intended to be a textbook but rather an enjoyable familiarization with Buddhism.

Nevertheless you cannot cut a straight line through the clouds if you hope to reach the essence of Buddhism. Buddhism has so many configurations that we must explore it culture to culture and sect to sect. That is why this book does not offer any particular school as the essence of Buddhism. They are all different but they are all important.

As a Christian who believes that Jesus is the Christ and the Savior of my life, I am not without my own presuppositions. As a Japanese-American whose cultural background is Buddhist, however, I am not without some sympathy and appreciation for the religion of my ancestors. Thus, I begin the dual quest to be both personal and objective.

This study begins with a portrait of my grandfather whose life was a Buddhist ideal for many people. After describing the life and times of the historical Buddha, Siddhartha Gautama, I discuss three major philosophies of Buddhism. Following that is a history of Buddhism in India, China, Tibet and Japan, and a look at Buddhist schools of thought which are significant to American society. Finally, I delineate the fundamental differences between Buddhism and Christianity and conclude with my own experiences in Japan.

This book would not have been possible without the assistance of many friends and the willingness of many people who shared with me their deep convictions about Buddhism. I especially want to mention the Spiritual Counterfeits Project (P.O. Box 4308, Berkeley, CA 94704) which allowed me the time to write this book. I also wish to express my appreciation to Koichi Ohtawa and Kenneth and Betty Roundhill who aided my research in Japan, and to Robert N. Minor who provided a technical critique of the manuscript. Finally I am grateful to God for my wife, Barbara, who encouraged me during the most difficult period of my writing.

ONE

Portrait of Grandfather

MY GRANDFATHER STOOD SILENTLY before the *Butsu-dan* in the living room, the center of the home. The *Butsu-dan* is a Buddha-shelf which is made of a special hard wood and is handed down the family line through the eldest son. It usually houses a bell, candles, two cups, a picture of a deceased family member and a Buddhist icon. They are placed randomly. At a *Butsu-dan*, appreciation is given to the departed and reverence is paid to the Buddha.

My grandfather bowed slowly to the picture in the *Butsu-dan*. After he poured fresh water into one cup and replaced the rice-ball in the other, he lit the candles and struck the bell twice with a padded stick. He offered an apple as usual; and today, he also presented a handful of yellow chrysanthe-mums to express his affection for the deceased. He stood back, bowed his head and clasped his hands. Between his thumbs and forefingers hung prayer beads. He silently prayed. Then he struck the bell, blew out the candles and bowed once more.

My grandfather was a devout Buddhist of the Jodo-shin school. After he settled in California, he helped start the Watsonville Buddhist Church. At times he was a cabinet official in the church; always he was devoted to the church and his faith. Although he was not an educated man, he read widely, especially the Buddhist scriptures. Once a month he read the Sutras to his children and related stories about the Buddha. Later in life, he spent considerable time printing Buddhist poetry on paper and wood. This was a special joy for him. He had a strong faith in Amida Buddha and was deeply committed to his religion. Because of his dedication, the Buddhist church changed his name after his death to Ingo, a special Buddhist name.

He came to America in 1906 from Yamaguchi-ken, Japan, where he had reluctantly left his wife who was pregnant with their first child. His original intention was to work and save money in America and then return to his family in Japan, but he never saw his homeland again. Instead, he sent for his wife and, after fourteen years, he sent for his daughter.

He was a farmer throughout his life, working with the earth from dawn to dust each day except Sunday when he would faithfully take his wife and eleven children to church. He was strict, but he was also quiet and gentle, rarely raising his voice to his children. Since he worked so much and had so many children, he could not spend much time with any one child. Nevertheless, one child was deaf and he did his best to help him financially with special schooling. He was generous with a good heart. He tried to raise his children not to drink, smoke or gamble. He never abandoned the traditional values of Japan and always upheld the ethics of the teachings of the Buddha.

He never learned English. He felt that he was too old to learn. He therefore never became an American citizen although he lived sixty-five of his ninety years in America. Perhaps this was one reason for the tragedy in his life.

Since he was not an American citizen, the United States government suspected his loyalty during the war with Japan. Three months after the Japanese attacked Pearl Harbor, the local police surrounded his home. Two FBI agents entered the house and ordered my grandfather out of bed. They didn't question him but they quickly escorted him away. He was taken to San Francisco, and a week later he was sent to prison in North Dakota. Because he was not a citizen, he was denied a trial.

Two months later my grandmother, father, uncles and aunts were sent to a relocation camp in Poston, Arizona. They received very little information about what was happening to my grandfather. After a year and a half, my grandfather was reunited with most of his family in Arizona. His oldest son was fighting for the Allies in France and Germany.

Although the government has never explained its treatment of my grandfather, no one ever heard him complain. From the teachings of the Buddha, he believed that his imprisonment had occurred because of his karma, and so he accepted it and bore no bitterness or malice toward anyone. Christian friends tried to share the gospel of Jesus Christ with him now and then. But he always told them that he didn't need to change his religion, for the teachings of the

Buddha had given him an ethical standard by which to live. Throughout his life he was a devout Buddhist who daily worshiped at the *Butsu-dan*, except during his imprisonment.

After his funeral, I sat on a couch in the living room with my relatives who were grieving over his death. I turned and looked at the orange chrysanthemums where my grandfather used to worship. There a new figure appeared. My grandmother had placed a picture of my grandfather in the *Butsu-dan*.

TWO

The Buddha

AS BUDDHISM SPREAD throughout Asia, Buddhists organized the religious precepts and practices inherent in a particular region into a coherent system of beliefs along with their own metaphysical presuppositions. For many, therefore, Buddhism is like the wandering grass which strengthens the hills and beautifies the meadows. It absorbs the rain of human thought and nourishes those who are spiritually hungry. So it was with my grandfather and so it has been for many for the past twenty-five centuries. And the first seed sprouted with the appearance of a man who has influenced an entire continent. His name is Siddhartha Gautama.

Siddhartha Gautama, the Historial Buddha

The biography of Siddhartha Gautama was not written during his lifetime.[1] The earliest available accounts of his life were collected some three hundred years after his death. Since then, both historical and legendary descriptions of his life have been included in the Pali Canon and in Sanscrit accounts. Historians have debated where to draw the line between history and legend, but no human mind can know what were the facts and what were not. Nevertheless, whether the stories of Gautama the Buddha be true or myth, his life has been and still is an inspiration and model for all Buddhists.

Over three thousand years ago the Aryan people wandered in several directions throughout Europe, the Middle East and South Asia. After conquering the Indus valley, the Aryans instituted Brahmanism and the caste system in the Indian culture, which enabled the invaders to maintain the purity of the Aryan blood and establish themselves as spiritual and social masters over the native Indians. The Brahman priests further centralized their power over all the castes and soon set up a religious monopoly for a privileged few.

In the sixth century B.C., innumerable sects and schools spontaneously exploded. One was Jainism, which was founded by Mahavira and has survived to this day. Another was the birth of Buddhism, which was to rival its parent as a major world religion. The founder of Buddhism was Gautama the Buddha, a contemporary of Mahavira and later interpreted as a long-awaited liberator.

Siddhartha Gautama[2] was probably born in 563 B.C. and died about eighty years later.[3] His father was King Suddhodana Gautama, a raja or chieftain of the Sakya clan, a family of the Kshatriya (warrior-nobility) caste of ancient Bharata.

His father reigned over Kapilavastu, a small region on the Indian slope of the Himalayas in the borderland between India and Nepal.

His mother was Maha Maya, who has been compared with Mary, Jesus' mother. According to some accounts, the Bodhisattva, or Buddha-to-be, chose her to be his own mother because of her faith and purity. While she slept, he took the form of a white elephant and entered her side. Maha Maya, thus, was blessed with the immaculate conception of the Buddha-to-be. Other accounts say that she dreamed this episode. In any case, after ten months of pregnancy, she gave birth to him in the Lumbini Gardens. Seven days after his birth she died, as mothers of Bodhisattvas normally do. Mahapajapati, his aunt and his father's second wife, assumed the task of rearing him.

At birth Gautama (his family name) received the name of Siddhartha, "he who has accomplished his objectives." He is also called Sakyamuni ("the wise sage of the Sakya clan"), Bhagavat ("blessed with happiness"), Tathagata ("the one who has gone thus"), Jina ("the victorious") and, of course, the Buddha ("the Enlightened One").

During his infancy, Siddhartha Gautama was visited by a sage, Asita,[4] who prophesied that Siddhartha would either become a great ruler like his father if he dwelt in his father's house, or he would become a Buddha, a remover of ignorance from the world if he went forth into the world. King Suddhodana knew that the sight of human misery would cause his son to leave home and to seek for truth. Since the king wanted his son to follow his footsteps to the throne, he issued strict orders to his subjects that the young prince was not to see any evil or suffering.

Meanwhile Gautama manifested supernatural intelligence

and strength as he grew up. At sixteen he secured the hand of his cousin, Yashodara,[5] by demonstrating twelve marvelous feats in the art of archery. Gautama may have had other wives, but Yashodara was his principal wife.

Despite the diligence of his father to sequester him from evil, Gautama eluded the royal attendants and drove his chariot four times through the city. On separate occasions he saw an old man, a leper, a corpse and an ascetic.[6] He realized from these four encounters that life was full of sorrows and that happiness was an illusion. Gautama thus became aware of human suffering.

Gautama left his family and kingdom on the same night in which Yashodara gave birth to his son Rahula.[7] The decision to leave was difficult for Gautama, but now that his son, whose name means "hindrance," was born and could continue the royal line, he could begin his spiritual quest for truth. He took his faithful servant Channa and his devoted horse Kanthaka as far as the forest, where he shaved off his hair and changed his robes. He left them there and began a pilgrimage of inquiry and asceticism.[8]

For six or seven years Gautama sought communion with the supreme cosmic spirit, first through the teachings of two Brahman hermits and then in the company of five monks. He practiced the traditional methods of asceticism such as fasting. Other physical austerities included sleeping on brambles to mortify the desires of his body and abstaining from sitting by crouching on his heels to develop his concentration. For long periods he ate nothing save a single grain of rice each day.

Despite all these efforts, Gautama did not succeed in attaining truth. Finally, he realized that his life as an ascetic was of no greater value than his previous life as a prince. Self-torture was vain and fruitless; privation was no better than pleasure. He understood, then, the importance of the Middle Way. Abandoning a life of extreme austerities, Gautama ate solid food. This act angered his fellow monks who thought that Gautama had weakened and succumbed to his physical needs. They promptly deserted him, thoroughly disgusted with Gautama's seeming worldliness.

On the wide bank of Meranjana at Gaya near the village of Uruvella, Gautama sat at the foot of a fig tree (commemorated as the Bodhi-tree). There Mara,[9] the evil one, determined to thwart Gautama from becoming the Buddha, enticing him with worldly temptations during his meditations. Gautama withstood all the challenges and experienced the revelation of liberating awareness—the way that provides escape from the cruel causality of samsara (the cycle of rebirths). Gautama discovered the Four Holy Truths which became known as *Pativedhanana*, the wisdom of Realization. Gautama henceforth was the Buddha, the Enlightened One.

After his Enlightenment, the Buddha was faced with a crucial decision. He could either renounce the world and withdraw with his knowledge, or he could remain with people and share the Four Holy Truths with those who sought deliverance from samsara. Out of his compassion for others, he chose the latter.

In the Deer Park at Rishipatana two months after he had been "awakened," the Buddha gave his first sermon or set in motion the Wheel of the Law, the symbol of the Buddhist faith and of the Buddha as well. There, he approached the five monks who had deserted him. At first they ignored him, but upon the realization that he had been enlightened, they sat and listened to his teachings and were converted. He received them into the Sangha, the mendicant order that has spread the Dharma (the doctrine of the Buddha) and the Vinaya (the disciplinary regulations concerning the conduct of the followers of the Buddha).

For more than forty years the Buddha dedicated himself to his ministry. Although he did not proselytize among the masses, he was concerned for others and was fired with a zealous sense of mission. The Sangha quickly grew. Many people were attracted to this man who was calm, reasonable, gentle, and who possessed a sense of humor. He embodied compassion. As the Buddha he could have withdrawn into a private world of fulfillment and bliss, but others had need of him. Therefore he became their teacher.

The Buddha was eighty when Cunda the blacksmith served him pig's flesh or, perhaps, mushrooms. He became very ill. Before he passed away, he sent a message to Cunda saying that he should not feel guilty for being the cause of his death, but that it was destined to be. The Buddha died at Kusinara (modern Kasia) in the district of Gorakhpur. Just before his death, he exhorted his disciples not to grieve. His last recorded words were: "Decay is inherent in all component things! Work out your own salvation with diligence."[10]

The Buddha probably never believed that he was a god but rather that he was an enlightened human being.

The Dharma, the Teachings of the Buddha

After the death of the Buddha, his disciples conducted their first council at Rajagrha, where they discussed his teachings. Much later, in 80 B.C., his teachings were compiled on paper and became the Pali Canon. These collections, called the *Tripitaka* (the three baskets), contain rules for conduct, methods for spiritual attainment and the ethics taught by the Buddha.

Like many of his contemporaries, the Buddha protested against the aristocratic religion of his day, first because it was corrupt and tyrannical, and second because it was too refined and intellectual for the common people. His teachings were open to all who would listen, and they were taught incisively and clearly so that they could be understood and experienced.

The religious tyranny of the Brahmans was uncompromising. The Brahmans held that the opportunity for the union of the individual soul with the Universal Soul (Brahman) was reserved for the sage caste and that only through numerous rebirths could lower castes enter into their caste. Since the hope of the Indian people was to someday become one with Brahman, this doctrine not only forced all other castes to submit to the rules of the Brahman priests in order to work their way to higher castes but it created an atmosphere of awe and fear of their authority.

Contrary to the prevailing Brahman doctrine, the Buddha recruited disciples from all castes. According to him, nirvana is extended to everyone who strictly obeys the laws of a monastic life, not withstanding their caste prior to conversion. The Buddha, however, did not seek to abolish the caste system. Instead, he believed that it was necessary for the framework of the temporal life. Since their lives were committed to the Dharma and the Sangha, only monks were exempt from caste distinctions. Nevertheless, however much he accepted the caste system sociologically, his doctrine was a giant step in reforming the religious corruption of his day.

The Buddha also reacted to the speculations of the Brahmans, who tried to assimilate the concept of Atman-Brahman (individual soul/Universal Soul) with the concept of samsara (rebirths or reincarnation) into a consistent and coherent system. The Buddha rejected such futile speculations because they hindered Enlightenment. He considered speculations vain and nonproductive.

Like Sankhya and Jainism, the Buddha rejected subservience to a supreme Lord, but unlike them he denied a belief in an eternal self. Furthermore, his concept of karma (the transcendental effect upon a person's life as a result of a person's actions accomplished in previous existences) has sometimes been misunderstood. Certainly he believed that karma determines the kind of rebirth, good or bad, according to past merit. The Buddha, however, did not believe that there is a self which is reborn but only a rearrangement of basic factors which are conventionally called the "self," like a "chariot" is a name for a certain grouping of parts, but not something other than that grouping or collection.

The Buddha also defined nirvana differently from the Brahmans. Whereas in Brahmanism, nirvana or *moksha* is attained when the individual soul realizes it is the Universal Soul, the Buddha held that nirvana is merely the termination of rebirths. Furthermore, he believed that nirvana is not immediately accessible, that several lives are required to attain it. He declared that, if nirvana depended only on the suppression of all feeling and thought, then the deaf, the blind and the insane could enter into it. He taught that the journey to nirvana is long and arduous, but that the fruits are the peace in living with all beings and the deliverance from samsara. Understandably, therefore, nirvana (which means "extinction" of suffering and rebirth) is the highest ideal to which a Buddhist aspires.

In the "Twelvefold Chain of Causation," the Buddha traced the cause of suffering to its origin. The following is a description of that process:

From ignorance as cause arise the aggregates (*sankhara*), from the aggregates as cause arises consciousness, from consciousness as cause arises name-and-form (mind and body), from name-and-form as cause arises the sphere of the six (senses), from the sphere of the six as cause contact, from contact as cause sensation, from sensation as cause craving, from craving as cause grasping, from grasping as cause becoming, from becoming as cause birth, from birth as cause arise old age, death, grief, lamentation, pain, dejection, and despair. Even so is the origination of all this mass of pain.[11]

The Buddha believed that suffering dominates the lives of all humanity, and he taught a practical way of deliverance from suffering. His teachings were collected into what forms the Dharma. The Four Holy Truths encapsulate his doctrines on suffering, and they are the heart of the Dharma.

The Four Holy Truths are essentially (1) the universality of suffering, (2) the origin of suffering, (3) the overcoming of suffering and (4) the way leading to the suppression of suffering. The first Truth defines the nature of being; the second and third Truths develop various aspects of being; and the fourth Truth indicates a way to practical deliverance.

The first Holy Truth is *Duhkha*. The Buddha taught that all people learn that life is grievous through the experience of birth, age and death. Contrary to the pantheism of Brahmanism, which taught that a divine thread is woven in all beings, the Buddha spoke of the self as a temporal creation cursed with suffering until deliverance is achieved.

The second Holy Truth is *Tanha*. The Buddha taught that suffering is caused by the false desires of the senses which have been deceived into clinging to the impermanent world. A hopeless quest for immortality further aggravates human pain, either because people are obsessed with survival or because people fear the failure of obtaining ultimate peace.

The third Holy Truth discusses how deliverance from suffering can be achieved. If the false desires of a changeable and perishable self cause suffering, then the desires need to be suppressed, abandoned or rejected in order to nullify their effects. Ignorance of the way of deliverance is the primordial cause of suffering. By understanding the Four Holy Truths deliverance can be secured.

The fourth Holy Truth is the Buddhist ethic. In it, the Buddha enumerates the Noble Eightfold Path. It is a sacred path with eight branches called: right views or understanding, right aspirations, right speech, right conduct or action, right livelihood, right effort or endeavor, right mind control or concentration, and right mindfulness. These eight branches are not stages which can be performed in succession or isolated from each other. Rather they are different dimensions of a total way of life. In the Dharma, the Buddha taught that suffering is the result of selfish desires and that they chain people to the wheel of insubstantial impermanent things. The Dharma aims at eliminating these selfish desires in ways described in the fourth Holy Truth and at guiding the individual to nirvana.

In his teachings, the Buddha ignored the worship of gods, but he did not deny their existence. To him the gods inhabit the cosmos and are impermanent like all other living beings. Thus, they too must escape rebirth through nirvana. The Buddha himself ironically has been revered above the gods. What was important to the Buddha, however, was not the worship of gods or himself but the following of his teachings.

Richard H. Robinson writes: "Gautama is reported to have said, 'What is there in seeing this wretched body? Whoever sees Dharma sees me; whoever sees me sees Dharma.' The immortality of the Buddha is that he is immanent in his Word."[12]

The Sangha, the Buddhist Monastic Order

The Sangha during the Buddha's lifetime was a Buddhist community of beggar-monks. They were not priests but they taught the way of deliverance through the examples of their lives. The Sangha originally consisted of groups of wandering mendicants. Today, however, Buddhist monks and nuns live in monasteries. The Sangha is also a term applied to a body of Buddhist believers.

The Buddha addressed his first sermon to the five monks near Benares. He continued to preach the Dharma to his followers rather than to the masses. This practice reflects the true nature of the Sangha at that time. If a person wanted to learn the Dharma and become a part of the Sangha, he had to become a beggar-monk.

Nevertheless, the Buddha did teach the Middle Way in which his followers abstained from self-torture as well as self-indulgence. They rejected luxury and they renounced the world, but they also reacted against the severe self-mortification of the contemporary holy men.

Each boy or man who wanted to be a postulant usually had to be at least fifteen. If he was accepted as a novice, his head was shaved to symbolize his renunciation of the world. He was then given a new name and a new robe. Finally he received the vows of a Buddhist monk. Later, after having completed his term as a novice and having been accepted into the order, he again was given a new name and a new robe. At any time, as a novice or a full-monk, he could return to lay life either temporarily or permanently.

Women had greater difficulty being accepted into the Sangha. The Buddha demonstrated a strong suspicion of women. In preaching against the physical temptations of the world, he denounced the sensual attraction which women exercised on men. The Buddha continually warned his disciples against the sinister guile of women.

When Ananda, his closest disciple, asked him, "How should we behave toward women?" the Buddha replied, "Not see them!"

"And if we have to see them?"

"Not speak to them!"

"And if we have to speak to them?"

"Keep your thoughts tightly controlled!"[13]

After long delay, the Buddha finally consented to have women accepted into the Sangha, but only accompanied by numerous restrictions. A nun was subject to the authority of a monk in all circumstances. "A nun," the Buddha laid down, "though she be a hundred years old must reverence a monk, rise on meeting him, salute him with clasped hands and honor him with her respects, although he may have been received into the order only that day."[14] The Buddha stated to Ananda that if women had not been received into the Order the Doctrine would have stayed for a thousand years; but since women have been accepted, the Doctrine will last only five hundred.[15]

The laity was permitted to follow the teachings of the Buddha while continuing to live in the world. Although they could receive heavenly rewards for aiding the monks in the Sangha, the laity could not attain nirvana or any of the higher fruits of the Dharma. They could receive one significant grace from their dedication to the Buddha and their generosity to the Sangha, and that was to be reborn as a person who will become a beggar-monk; for only total renunciation of the world leads to deliverance.

The Buddha, the Dharma and the Sangha are referred to as the "Three Jewels" of Buddhism.

THREE

Philosophies of Buddhism

A SYSTEMATIC BUDDHIST THEOLOGY apparently was not put in written form until four centuries after the Buddha's death. Consequently schisms occurred within the Sangha during those centuries over the content of the Dharma. By the close of the third century B.C., the Buddhists were separated into no less than eighteen schools. Three major branches of Buddhism eventually developed into Hinayana (the Little Vehicle), Mahayana (the Great Vehicle) and Vajrayana (the Tantric Vehicle).[1] Yana means "vehicle" or "the way of progress." Thus, through yana the Buddhist crosses the river of rebirth and arrives upon the shore of nirvana.[2]

Theravada Buddhism

The Buddha was primarily concerned with deliverance from samsara (death and rebirth) and the path which leads to nirvana (the extinction of the individual soul). He did not try to establish a new religion nor construct an elaborate philosophy. Instead he taught his disciples a discipline which was based on the Four Holy Truths and the Noble Eightfold Path.

Early Buddhism at once contained strength and weakness. As a discipline, early Buddhism accommodated itself to most religious philosophies throughout Asia; this probably was the chief reason for the wide expansion of Buddhism in the East. As a discipline, however, early Buddhism did not provide a refined, unified system of beliefs and practices; this was perhaps a major cause for the inevitable triumph of Hinduism over Buddhism in India.

Schisms continually rocked early Buddhism and subdivided the Sangha into numerous schools and sects. The wide variety of beliefs and practices among the many schools further facilitated the spread of Buddhism, but it also blunted its ability to compete successfully with Hinduism.

Since the words of the Buddha were not recorded during his lifetime, the transmission of the Dharma depended on the memory of his disciples and their understanding of what he meant. The traditional Theravada account is that in 477 B.C.,[3] Kashyapa, the leading monk at that time, assembled a council of the disciples of the Buddha in Rajagriha. During the meeting Kashyapa questioned Ananda concerning the Buddha's discourses. Ananda's answers constitute the Sutras. Also during the meeting, Upali is questioned on practical affairs of the Sangha. His answers constitute the Vinaya.

The Buddhist schools responded to and interpreted the

Sutras and the Vinaya differently. Two major philosophies soon emerged within Buddhism, Theravada and Mahayana Buddhism. The adherents of Mahayana Buddhism soon referred to those Buddhists who held strictly to the letter of the Buddhist doctrine as followers of Hinayana Buddhism, the Little or Lesser Vehicle. The Hinayanists resented this term because it denoted an inferior method of Buddhism. Instead they called their doctrine Theravada Buddhism, the doctrine of the Elders.[4]

Theravada Buddhism is said to be the fundamentalist branch of Buddhism because it has preserved most of the original nature of Buddhism. By the first century B.C., Buddhist scriptures were collected and written in the Pali language, a vernacular descended from Sanskrit. These scriptures became known as the Pali Canon and the foundation of Theravada beliefs and practices. The Theravadins believe that the Pali Canon is an accurate account of what the Buddha taught even though they acknowledge that a number of discourses in the Pali Canon belong solely to several of his disciples.

Theravada Buddhism contains major points of doctrine which differ from the beliefs of most Mahayana schools. Most significantly the Theravadins revere the Buddha as a great ethical teacher, but not as a god as many of the Mahayanists do. Furthermore, their teachings are reserved for the Buddhist saints and not for the common people, another departure from many of the Mahayana schools. Nirvana is also limited to those select few who practice the rigid disciplines which are taught in the Pali scriptures.

Buddhaghosa is unquestionably the foremost commentator of Theravada Buddhism. The Buddhists of South and Southeast Asia regard him as the Father of their religion.

Buddhaghosa was born into a Brahman family in the latter half of the fourth century A.D. He converted to Buddhism and traveled to Ceylon (modern Sri Lanka) where he compiled an extensive encyclopedia of Pali Buddhist literature which retains its authority today.

Theravada Buddhism has been firmly planted in Sri Lanka. Its fate, however, in other countries of Southeast Asia has been similar to its demise in India. For a time the Theravadins were in Indonesia, but the persecution from the Moslems and Hindus eventually drove them out of that country in the fifteenth and sixteenth centuries. In this century communism has restricted the teachings and practice of all religions within Vietnam, Cambodia, Laos and other areas in Southeast Asia.

Although Theravada Buddhism can only claim a small following, it still survives. Although it has suffered at the hands of other religions and philosophical doctrines, it does enjoy a friendly relationship with Mahayana Buddhism. The reason for this camaraderie among Buddhists is that, generally speaking, they have a tolerant attitude toward doctrine. So long as each is loyal to the essential spirit of the Buddha, each may embrace in fellowship as Buddhists.

Mahayana Buddhism

Beatrice Suzuki described an important difference in the emphasis between the two philosophies of Buddhism, a difference which occurred in Buddhism about two thousand years ago when Mahayana evolved as a new and separate Buddhist movement:

When the Buddha obtained Enlightenment under the Bodhi-tree two courses were open to him: one, to keep his knowledge to himself and to pass into the bliss of Nirvana;

the other, prompted by compassion for other beings to remain in the world to bestow the benefits of his wisdom upon all. These two ways mark the difference between Hinayana and Mahayana, for while Hinayana does not by any means ignore compassion for others, nevertheless it stresses individual enlightenment. Mahayana, on the other hand, while not neglecting wisdom, nevertheless stresses compassion to such a marked degree that it over-shadows the Hinayana in this aspect of Buddhism.[5]
The central goal of the Mahayana Buddhist is not merely to achieve personal deliverance from samsara (death and re-birth) and karma (causal retribution), as the Theravadins do, but to assist others in the quest for deliverance as well.

This, however, does not mean that the Mahayanists are indifferent to their own enlightenment. Says Suzuki, "What is most important in Mahayana is Enlightenment, freedom from Illusion, and the aspiration after Buddhahood, and this not for a few wise monks but for all beings."[6] The key word is "all." The Mahayana philosophy seeks deliverance not only for the saint but for everyone, and it is this extension of the compassion of the Buddha which sets the Mahayana apart from the Theravada, thereby establishing a new and richer Buddhist ethic.

In spite of this difference, the canons in both the Little and the Great Vehicle substantially overlap. The Theravadin scriptures are composed of the Sutta (Sutras, discourses and biography of Gautama the Buddha), Vinaya (rules for the discipline of the Sangha) and Abhidhamma (analysis and exposition of doctrine). The Mahayanist scriptures consist of much of the Pali writings, as well as other works which are considered scriptural according to various, respective schools.

The early Mahayanists contended that their scriptures outside the Pali Canon were also of ancient origin. They say that those works which were later revealed had been secretly concealed from the time of the Buddha until his followers as a whole could understand them. The Mahayanists certainly did not reject the Pali Canon but did regard it as incomplete. They subscribed to the belief of a continually developing revelation. Since the Buddha had privately taught these hidden principles to a select few, others had to disclose them to the general following at the appropriate time.

Other defenders of Mahayana Buddhism state that the Buddha did not teach esoteric doctrines, but that he freely shared both Theravadin and Mahayanist principles. They assert that the compilers of the Pali Canon, who had endorsed the Theravadin doctrine, omitted teachings which were to become the foundation of the Mahayana philosophy.

The Mahayanists maintain that the Buddha had never desired that his teachings should become complete in themselves, but that they be seeds in the minds of those who would share the fruits of their insights grown from his teachings. Thus, the Mahayanists state that while Theravada Buddhism upholds the letter of the Dharma, Mahayana Buddhism captures the true spirit of the Middle Way.

As Mahayana Buddhism became increasingly popular among the masses, it abandoned the seemingly atheistic doctrines of Theravada Buddhism, which had no omnipotent God who intervenes to deliver people from samsara and karma. The Mahayanists, however, allowed the possibility of divine intercession, which eventually resulted in the deification of the Buddha. Ironically, after he was elevated to the position of God, he was depersonalized and was relegated to be one of a myriad of Buddhas as centuries passed.

Nevertheless, the Buddha became more than a great teacher to the Mahayanists; he became their personal savior. Their longing for a divine friend and a supreme god was fulfilled in him. Furthermore, metaphysical questions which the Buddha has seemingly refused to discuss as unprofitable could now be explained.

The *Trikaya*, the three bodies of the Buddha, is at the heart of Mahayana Buddhism. After the historical Buddha became a Supreme Being, naturally his roles were extended. Thus the Mahayanists thought of the Buddha as (1) Nirmanakaya (the historical Buddha), the *sakyamuni* who lived on earth in human form, (2) Sambhogakaya (the eternal Buddha), the Buddha ideal as exemplified in the Amida of the Pure Land schools,[7] and (3) Dharmakaya (the Universal Buddha), "the permanent, undifferentiated, comprehending Truth,"[8] which can be realized only through mystical experience such as taught in the Shingon.[9] The *Trikaya* threads its way throughout all the teachings of the Mahayana; and, although different schools interpret it differently and emphasize one character of the Buddha over the others, they all believe in the three bodies of the Buddha.

The doctrine of the Bodhisattva was introduced into Mahayana Buddhism to enhance the mercy of the Buddha by aiding in the Enlightenment of others. In Theravada Buddhism, believers are instructed to become Arhats, Buddhist saints who have achieved their own deliverance from samsara. In Mahayana Buddhism, converts are taught to become Bodhisattvas, great beings who are destined for Buddhahood but who delay this goal to help others. The difference between these two Buddhist doctrines is that the Arhat focuses upon his own Enlightenment while the Bodhisattva seeks liberation from suffering for all creatures.

The Bodhisattva stores up a vast amount of merit through numerous lives of self-sacrifice. This amount is more than enough to make him a Buddha. Consequently he can distribute excess merit to those who call on him in sincere faith. Thus, believers are reborn in paradise, not through their own merits, but through those of the Bodhisattva. What is crucial, however, is that the Bodhisattva must postpone his entrance into nirvana in order to help others achieve theirs. By doing so, he saves them from countless miseries and afflictions. It is therefore understandable why the Bodhisattvas became living symbols of compassion and the central ideal of Mahayana philosophy.

Another important feature of Mahayana Buddhism resides in the exceptional quality of its thinkers. Its twofold participation in the Wheel of the Law are in the second and third turns, the Buddha having fulfilled the first turn.

The teachings of Nagarjuna, the great philosopher of the first and second centuries A.D., accomplished the second turn. He also established the Madhyamika, the first major school of the Mahayana. He said that life is relative and described the supreme reality as *Sunyata* or the Void. He expounded the doctrine of the emptiness of all views of form and taught that intuitive understanding of the true meaning of the Void is true wisdom.

In the early fifth century, the famous philosopher Asanga developed a doctrine which initiated the third turn. He established the Yogacara, the second major school of the Mahayana. He preached that the external world is illusionary and deceptive. He did not refer to the world as "absolute emptiness" (as his predecessor had done) but as the extension of man's consciousness. He taught that the only reality is the mind and that the world is an extension of it.

The philosophical doctrines of Nagarjuna, Asanga and other Mahayanist thinkers had a tremendous impact on Buddhism which moved the Theravada and the Mahayana further apart. Their ideas may have caused strong, swift currents to rush in separate directions; the followers of the Buddha, however, believe that Buddhism is a large enough ocean to contain the seas of every Buddhist thought. Theravadins and Mahayanists may disagree as to the nature of nirvana, yet they all believe that it is attainable whether it be through Arhatship or Bodhisattvaship.

Nevertheless, a pilot may sail the same ocean as his brother but still regard his brother's ship as an inferior vessel. So too do the Mahayanists regard the Theravadin doctrine of nirvana to be negative and inferior. The Theravadin vessel may lead to nirvana, but if it does, and Mahayanists doubt that in this latter age, it does so in a way that is negative in which not to do evil is stressed more than to do good. The Bodhisattva, in contrast, steers the Mahayanist vessel in an act of supreme mercy and compassion.

Beatrice Suzuki, an advocate for Mahayana Buddhism, describes the difference in this way: "Mahayana means 'great vehicle,' in contrast to Hinayana's 'small vehicle.' The idea is that the Mahayana carriage or vehicle is large enough to carry all beings to salvation, while the small carriage of Hinayana can only carry the few."[10]

Vajrayana Buddhism

The Vajrayana or Adamantine Vehicle is often classified as a school of Mahayana Buddhism. Because it is so different from the rest of Buddhism in doctrine and practice, and because it monopolizes certain regions and peoples, however, Vajrayana Buddhism can reasonably be considered to be a Buddhist philosophy in its own right.

The Vajrayana was born in India probably in the seventh century A.D., although followers of this vehicle would argue a much earlier date of birth. The Vajrayana later became the religion of Tibet and Mongolia. It soon was recognized as Tibetan Buddhism or Lamaism. Tibetan Buddhists liken the Vajrayana to a diamond because they consider both to be precious, changeless, pure and clear. Says Lama Anagarika Govinda, "The *vajra* is regarded as the symbol of highest spiritual power which is irresistible and invincible. It is therefore compared to the diamond, which is capable of cutting asunder any other substance, but which itself cannot be cut by anything."[11]

Even more syncretistic than the Mahayana, the Vajrayana absorbed the Tantrism which had made inroads into Hinduism. Since Tantrism is such a vital element of its doctrine, Vajrayana Buddhism became known as Tantric Buddhism. Tibetan Buddhists claim that early Buddhism contained Tantric tendencies which date back to the first century A.D., and that the Hindus borrowed Tantric ideas from Buddhism. Most scholars, however, believe that Tantrism was a fruit of Indian Hinduism.

In the sixth century A.D., a number of spiritual books appeared in the religious circles of Indian life. They were referred to as *Tantras*. The word *tantra* relates to weaving. Thus, the theme of Tantrism is the interwovenness, the interdependence and the oneness of all things. Tantrism is a mystical belief system which incorporates magical procedures in the attainment of supernatural powers. In Tantric Buddhism these powers are employed in the quest for Enlightenment.

Practitioners of Tantrism utilize the mind, speech and body in their meditation. Technical aids are mantras, yantras

and mudras. Tantric Buddhists attribute considerable importance to the mantra as the audio technique of meditation.
They believe that the sacred syllables of a mantra have the
power to penetrate the Absolute and communicate with
divine spirits, or rather the Buddhas and the Bodhisattvas.
Their most sacred mantra is *Om Mani Padme Hum.*

The yantra is the visual technique of meditation. The most
important visual is the mandala which displays an intricate
pattern of symbolic figures. The Buddhist mandala reveals
to the meditator secret forces which emanate from within
his own consciousness through the figures of peaceful and
wrathful deities, or rather the Buddhas and the Bodhisattvas.[12] The mandala is at once a symbolic representation
of the human body and the entire universe.

The mudras are bodily gestures which accompany meditation. The hand gestures are particularly significant. The
positions of hands and fingers distinguish the identity of
the Buddhas and the Bodhisattvas from one another who
each represent a distinct spiritual quality.[13]

The total dedication to the quest for Enlightenment
through the use of Tantrism is known as the Short Path.
The Short Path employs techniques to reach Enlightenment
much more quickly through far fewer lifetimes than would
be otherwise accomplished through Mahayana practices.
Since spiritual aids in Tantrism are so powerful and danger-
ous, Tibetan Buddhists urge that they be used only under
the instruction and guidance of a trained Lama or yogin.
"Devotees entering upon the Short Path," says John Blofeld,
"are taught that henceforth they must do more than practice
virtue and eschew evil."[14] In other words, they must go
beyond the Mahayana code of conduct and enlist special
Tantric techniques such as mantras, yantras and mudras to

attain Enlightenment in their lifetime. The Eightfold Path of the Buddha subsequently became secondary to the Short Path of Tantrism for many Vajrayana Buddhists.

Another significant doctrine which the Vajrayana absorbed was Shaktism, a Hindu belief-system which worshiped the divine power of the consort of a particular god. Translated into the Vajrayana doctrine, Shaktism attributed each Buddha and lesser god with female counterparts. The Tibetan gods became the symbol of *upaya*. *Upaya* (literally, "skillful means") is love and compassion; it is the active, male principle. The Tibetan goddesses became the symbol of *prajna*. *Prajna* is knowledge; it is the passive, female principle. The union of *upaya* and *prajna* became the spiritual symbol for achieving nirvana.[15]

The extent to which a Tibetan Buddhist takes this concept literally is the extent to which he is engaged in Shaktism. Many Vajrayana Buddhists regard this important doctrine as a symbolic expression of the oneness of body and spirit and the union between supreme bliss and wisdom. They disdain any reference to Tibetan Buddhism as being a form of Shaktism. For them, *upaya* and *prajna* must unite in order for a person to attain perfect Buddhahood, but that person must not abuse this principle by engaging in sexual promiscuity.

Other Vajrayana Buddhists consider the union of *upaya* and *prajna* to mean sexual union. They document their belief from the literal application of Anangavajra's "Prajnopaya-viniscayasiddhi" which exhorts believers to enjoy all women. They believe that sexual union with a woman during sacred rituals will accelerate the attainment of Perfection.

It is not to say that the former group rejects sexual practice as a spiritual aid, but that the latter group has twisted the motivation from ego-destroying to ego-satiating. The same can be said of magic and the occult. All Vajrayana Buddhists accept magic and the occult as spiritual tools in attaining Enlightenment, but the motivation and therefore the end depend on the individual.

In either case, the Vajrayana is a far departure from the Theravada both in the doctrine of the deity of the Buddha and in the consideration of women. Like other Mahayana schools, the Vajrayana denies any consideration between the seemingly atheistic doctrine of the Buddha and the later doctrines which bestowed divine attributes to him. Instead they dismiss the paradox as a superficial observation, stating "that the Buddha, who is worshipped, is not the historical personality of the man Siddhartha Gautama, but the embodiment of the divine qualities, which are latent in every human being and which became apparent in Gautama as in innumerable Buddhas before him."[16]

The belief in female divinities, however, is not only a contradiction of the Buddha's supposed atheism but antithetical to the Buddha's attitude toward women as narrated in early scriptures. Recall that the Buddha distrusted women and that only after delay and misgivings did he admit them into the order. Furthermore, he decreed that they be subjugated to the lowest level of the Sangha. When Ananda asked his reasons for his hostility, the Buddha answered, "women are evil, Ananda, women are jealous, envious, stupid."[17]

Again, however, both Mahayana and Vajrayana Buddhists dismiss these accounts of the Buddha's antipathy toward women as a corruption of the texts and a false rendering of his teachings. Also the argument that Buddhism is an evolving religion, and that the teachings of the Buddha are becoming clearer with time, is employed to resolve this seeming contradiction. Therefore what may seem to be a far departure from the Buddha's original teachings to the Theravadins and others is certainly not to the Vajrayana Buddhists.

The addition of Tantrism and Shaktism to Buddhism might be considered the last turn of the Dharma. Undoubtedly they gave a new twist to Buddhism and became essential to the doctrine of the Vajrayana just as the prayer-wheel became essential to the lifestyle of the Vajrayana Buddhist, for prayer-wheels are to the Tibetan Buddhist as wheels are to a vehicle.

The prayer-wheel is *mani-cho-khor* in Tibetan Buddhism. It is a cylinder which is embossed with the mantra, *Om Mani Padme Hum*. It also has a little bell which rings with each revolution. It symbolically reflects the turning of the Wheel of the Dharma, in which the Buddha effected the first turn. Its purpose is to aid the meditator in concentrating on his mantra. Says Lama Anagarika Govinda, "The *mani-khor-eo* [another name for the prayer-wheel] is an expression of supreme faith in the infinite power of goodwill and love that may act through an infinite number of means."[18] The prayer-wheel is an exotic and unique symbol of the Vajrayana philosophy, which has contributed much to Buddhism.

FOUR

The History of Buddhism

AT THE END OF HIS LIFE, Gautama the Buddha did not send his disciples out to proselytize the world, as Jesus later did. Nevertheless, by the time of Christ's birth, the teachings of the Buddha had spread throughout much of Asia. Perhaps this was due to the character of the Buddha who had dedicated his life to the sharing of the Dharma. For whatever reason, Buddhism eventually became an integral part of the major cultures of Asia for many centuries.

India

Westerners have often referred to Gautama the Buddha as "the Christ of Hinduism," since he struggled against the injustices of the established religion of his day and since he became the founder and god of a new religious faith. Easterners might reverse the phrase and say that Jesus Christ was "the Buddha of Judaism." Certainly both men have won the hearts of generations of peoples.

Other similarities might be drawn between Buddhism and Christianity. Buddhism had to overcome the fierce hostility of its parent Hinduism, just as Christianity had to with its parent Judaism. Both Hinduism and Judaism, as the established religions, attempted to banish what they regarded as heretical sects. Furthermore, the ruling authorities in both parts of the world severely persecuted each respectively until a later emperor decreed it a state religion. The ruler who favored Buddhism was King Asoka (274-236 B.C.). He was the third emperor of the Maurya dynasty in India, and he has been referred to as "the Constantine of Buddhism."

Early in his reign Asoka was an ambitious conqueror who extended his power over much of the Indian peninsula. This ambition caused him to set his sights on Kalinga which had tenaciously opposed Mauryan rule. In 260 B.C., he attacked and defeated the forces of Kalinga. After the fighting, however, he became deeply grieved over the carnage and bloodshed of the battle.

The gentleness and compassion of Buddhism gave him solace for the guilt of his crimes. After he sought penitence in Buddhism, he studied the Dharma and traveled on a pilgrimage to Bodhgaya. Later Asoka instituted Buddhism as the state religion.

Asoka astutely adopted Buddhism for political advantage along with his spiritual convictions. Since his rule over South Asia was undisputed after the war with Kalinga, and since he had peaceful relations with Persia, his only strong neighbor, he now could afford to initiate a reign of nonviolence. "His problem was to consolidate a heterogeneous assortment of tribes and people into one cultural community," says Richard H. Robinson. "To achieve this end, he sought an ideological common denominator, and utilized all the available means of communication to propagate it."[1] The common denominator was Buddhism.

Around 245 B.C., Asoka assembled the third Buddhist council which finally established a definitive canon. Under his rule, he also commissioned Buddhist missionaries to spread the teachings of the Buddha into foreign lands, possibly as far as Syria, Egypt and Greece. This evangelism was successful in South and Southeast Asia, particularly in Ceylon. Mahinda, who may have been closely related to Asoka, introduced Buddhism to Ceylon, where Buddhism has continued in perhaps a purer form than anywhere else for two thousand years despite the presence of Mahayana and Tantric elements of Buddhism. Much credit, however, must go to Asoka for the diffusion of Buddhism because of his missionary vision and zeal.

During the Gupta dynasty (A.D. 300-650), Buddhism apparently enjoyed its greatest success in India. Nevertheless, despite the popularity of Buddhism at this time, Hinduism had far from disappeared from the scene. A Brahman revival had occurred in India about the second century B.C. From then on, the Brahmans commenced an aggressive campaign against Buddhism. In the following centuries, Buddhism experienced periods of growth and persecutions even during the Gupta dynasty.

At the end of the Gupta dynasty, the White Hun invasion destroyed many Buddhist monasteries such as the ones in Gandhara. In the eighth century, the reformation of Hinduism facilitated the progressive disappearance of Buddhism from Indian life. By the ninth century, Buddhism only flourished in those places where the state gave it special privileges, such as in Kashmir.

In 1193, Mohammed Bakhtyai razed Buddhist monasteries to the ground and massacred Buddhist monks. As a consequence of the Moslem invasion, Buddhism finally ended its career in India after fifteen centuries.

There are many possible reasons why Buddhism experienced an unhappy fate in India while thriving in most other Asian countries; none of these reasons are universally accepted. One reason is the attitude of the Buddhist clergy which maintained a passive stance in relation to Hinduism by preaching the Middle Way. Because of its principle of tolerance, Buddhism gradually became Hinduized in India. Thus, it lacked a reason for having a separate existence. Contrary to this argument, however, Mahayana Buddhism was particularly hostile to the theistic schools of Hinduism. Rivalry among Buddhist, Jain and Hindu sects also seems to have been stronger than the spirit of conciliation.

Another possible reason is that the Buddhists were victims of numerous bloody persecutions, first by the Brahmans, then by the Moslems. A third reason which has been proposed is that the historical Buddha became either a legend or merely another Hindu god to many of the Indians with the passing of time. The Mahayana concept of the Bodhisattvas reinforced this belief as the Bodhisattvas merged more and more with the Brahman gods in the eyes of the Indians.

Richard H. Robinson states another reason for the demise of Buddhism in India. Buddhism had become an institution in India which "had grown self-centered, conservative, and unresponsive to the needs of the people. The great monasteries depended not on widows' mites but on landed estates and royal grants, so they neglected to maintain popular support, ... when the monasteries lost royal support, or were destroyed by invasions, the general populations had little interest in either preserving the Dharma or restoring the Sangha."[2]

Probably all of these reasons, as well as others, contributed to the overall removal of Buddhism from its homeland. Today the number of Buddhists in India is small; most of them inhabit North Bengal where Tibetan influence has preserved Buddhism. Nevertheless, by the time Buddhism had departed from India, it had entered and become an essential part of the religious framework of many other Asian countries.

China

The three major religions which have played key roles in shaping the history of China are Confucianism, Taoism and Buddhism. Since Buddhism was the last to be introduced, the story of its development in China cannot be told apart from an understanding of the other two.

Confucius taught an ethical doctrine which had its roots in the ancient traditions of China and which included his own thoughts on piety and conduct. His followers developed his teachings further into what became Confucianism. Lao Tzu is reputedly the founder of Taoism, a philosophy which explained humanity's relationship with the world and the universe in mystical terms. Buddhism migrated from India into China in the first century A.D. and completed China's religious family.

Many Chinese Communists, including Mao Tse-tung, have been vocal in their hostility toward Confucius as representing the old Chinese tradition. For centuries, however, the Chinese have revered Confucius as "the Chinese ideal," or the prototype of the Chinese gentleman (*chun tzu*). Certainly he was one of the greatest religious and moral reformers in all of history.

During his lifetime, however, Confucius (551-479 B.C.) never received the veneration of the Chinese people. Although he fought ceaselessly to reform the political corruption of his day with a strong ethical code, the rulers of various districts of China either ignored or banished him so that he was only able to channel his thoughts through the teaching of his disciples. His primary ambition was to work for a better change in government, but since he did not live to see the effects of his work on his society, he regarded himself as a failure on his deathbed.

Confucius believed that the social environment was a result of the character of the ruler and that the condition of society molded the individual. Thus, Confucius taught that if a ruler is good and just the people will be virtuous and obedient, and that if the ruler is cruel and exacting, the people will be rebellious and self-centered. "If you showed a sincere desire to be good, your people would likewise be good," he boldly said to Baron Chi K'ang Tsu. "The virtue of the prince is like unto wind; that of the people like unto grass. For it is the nature of grass to bend when the wind blows upon it."[3]

Debate still rages on whether Confucius saw human nature as good or evil. Mencius, the great Confucian philosopher of the fourth century B.C., viewed human nature as good. Hsun Tzu, "the moulder of ancient Confucianism,"[4] said that human nature was evil. In any case, Confucius and his followers all believed that education could cultivate the highest virtues in man and that happiness could be achieved for everyone in a society ruled by a good government.

Thus, Confucius believed that the human condition could be socially determined and that universal happiness could be attained through social reform. His was an optimistic philosophy with a strong emphasis on social justice. Confucius said that a person should feel no shame at "wearing shabby clothes and eating poor food" (*Analects* 4.9), while elsewhere he said, "but one should feel deeply ashamed if he does nothing to alleviate the poverty of the common people."[5]

Furthermore, Confucius changed the meaning of "the Chinese gentleman." Before Confucius, *chun tzu* had denoted "a man of good birth, whose ancestors had belonged to a stratum above that of the common herd. . . . Confucius, on the contrary, asserted that any man might be a gentleman, if his conduct were noble, unselfish, just, and kind."[6]

The Confucian canon includes the Five Classics and the Four Books. The Classics (the books of Poetry, History, Changes, Rites, and the Annals of Spring and Autumn) were written before or during the time of Confucius. The *I Ching* (the book of Changes) is a handbook on divination. It became one of the Classics during the Han dynasty (202 B.C.— A.D. 220), "despite the fact that Confucius and all the great early Confucians had scorned the practice of divination."[7]

The Four Books (*Analects, Mencius, Great Learning* and *Doctrine of the Mean*) are believed to be the writings of his later followers. They were established as sacred scriptures during the Sung dynasty (960-1279).

In the *Analects*, Confucius is said to have a different understanding of the ancient word *tao* than the Taoists. He did not view the *Tao* as mystically as they did, but rather as a path to happiness for the individual and society. The path varies with each person, but for each the motivation must be centered on justice and appropriate love for everyone, particularly the family. A moral standard in the context of the family and the state was developed from this teaching. Later it would stand in conflict with the Theravadin philosophy which considered the monastic and celibate life to be the only path to salvation and perfection.

Nevertheless, as wise and incisive as Confucius was in his teachings, "he made no claim to the possession of the ultimate truth."[8] Although he seemed to have believed in a moral force in the universe and even a personal God called T'ien, he never incorporated his religious beliefs about God into his discussion on moral ethics.

Older than Confucianism, historical scholars still debate the emergence of Taoism in China. The principle of the *Tao* certainly was central to Chinese thought long before the Taoist school established itself as a mystical religion. The Taoists regard Lao Tzu ("old master"), supposedly of the sixth century B.C., as the father of Taoism. He is also credited with the *Tao Te Ching* ("The Book of the Virtuous Way"). Most scholars agree, however, that Lao Tzu is a legendary figure.

The *Tao* cannot truly be expressed in words, primarily because its meaning is extremely different to different people. Confucius spoke of the *Tao* as an ethical concept, a way of action. Meanwhile, the Taoists spoke of the *Tao* in metaphysical terms, exhorting individuals to become mystically one with the way of Nature—the absolute primal state, and thereby being one with the *Tao*. As the Taoists seek harmony with the *Tao*, they must reconcile yin and yang, the dual qualities of all life. Yin and yang are principles of change: yin is the female, passive principle; yang is the male, active principle. When they are in right balance, the Taoists can achieve harmony with the "Way."

Although passive and reflective in their inner meditation, Taoists seek cosmic power as well as enlightenment. Consequently Taoism eventually absorbed magic and sorcery. Their emphasis on mystical experience and the search for immortality contrasted with the scholarly pursuits of the Confucianists.

While Taoism and Confucianism attracted people of different temperaments, Buddhism came and fused with both of them. Buddhism complemented Taoism more quickly than it did Confucianism. It enriched Taoist ideas and strengthened Taoist doctrines. The Buddhists readily accepted Taoist concepts and terms, even including Taoist deities in their temples. The Taoists themselves, however, were often hostile to this new religion.

The seeds of Buddhism were sown in China with tremendous difficulty. The Chinese, particularly at first, objected to it because they considered it barbarous. "The Chinese had long considered themselves the most cultured, the most important, and indeed the only really important people on the face of the earth," says H. G. Creel. "They believed all other peoples to be 'barbarians.' "[9] Although Confucianism and Taoism absorbed much of Mahayana Buddhism, conservative Chinese have always regarded Buddhism as a foreign doctrine.

Notwithstanding the religious prejudice of the Chinese, there were doctrinal points in Buddhism which conflicted with traditional Chinese thought. The Chinese doubted reincarnation, an essential concept in Buddhism. The Chinese also stressed the importance of the family. Therefore

53

they strongly opposed the monastic life taught by the Buddhists, especially the Theravadists. Furthermore the Chinese, as well as the Japanese, "have cultivated an aesthetic appreciation of Nature, which apart from Buddhist and Taoist influences, has reached such heights of satisfaction as to make the Far Easterner want to prolong life in this world as long as possible," says John Noss.[10] This attitude toward Nature and life conflicts dramatically with Indian views that Nature is impermanent, unimportant or even illusionary, and with Gautama's teaching that life is suffering.

The Confucians initially resisted Buddhism even more than the Taoists. The orthodox Confucians particularly disliked the Buddhist preoccupation with metaphysics rather than with social concerns. Buddhism not only seemed nihilistic to them, but they felt that it compelled people to concentrate on self-salvation rather than on one's role and responsibility to society.

During the first century, the Han dynasty (202 B.C.—A.D. 220) established a peaceful order in Central Asia. This atmosphere of tranquillity enabled Theravada, and perhaps even Mahayana, Buddhism to wander and sprout throughout mainland Asia. Prior to the Han dynasty, very little outside influence penetrated the Chinese civilization. They were isolated from the rest of the world and were content to remain hidden. Buddhism, however, opened the doors and changed the religious and cultural way of life in China.

For several centuries China had been a quagmire of warring districts and feuding lords with impotent emperors as her titular heads. Finally the ruler of the state of Ch'in was able to secure military control over all of China and establish the Legalist system of autocratic rule in 221 B.C.[11] The Ch'in dynasty was so harsh that rebellion, along with inner political rivalry after the death of the Lord of Ch'in, quickly toppled the government.

The first peasant to sit on the Chinese throne soon established the Han dynasty. Han Kao Tsu favored Confucianism because he knew that its popularity with the people would secure their loyalty. Tsu's court, however, was not exclusively Confucian in outlook as other religious influences appeared in his government.

Many Chinese converted to Buddhism during the Han dynasty both because Buddhism was new and mystical and because Confucianism seemed too formal in its ritual and ceremony. The Chinese also were attracted to the serenity and gentleness of Buddhism. Furthermore, the multiplicity of doctrinal possibilities within Buddhism enabled it to appeal to people of different temperaments.

The success of Buddhism during this period is ironic because under the Emperor Wu (140-87 B.C.), the sixth ruler of the Han dynasty, Confucianism was finally adopted as the official philosophy of the state. Upon closer study, however, Wu drifted further and further away from the Confucian religion so that during most of his reign he lauded it in public to placate the people, but ignored it in private.

Nevertheless, for the past two millennia until the Communist takeover, Confucianism has maintained a high position in Chinese society with few interludes of disfavor. Meanwhile, Chinese Buddhism has experienced a history of successes and setbacks.

The Han dynasty crumbled at the hands of the Tartars who invaded China in the third century. Because of the patronage of the Tartar kings and the turbulence of the period up until the sixth century, Buddhism was able to root deeply into the Chinese soil.

Under the Tang dynasty (A.D. 618-906), China was again unified. Buddhism enjoyed its strongest influence at the royal court at this time. By now, Mahayana had become the predominant Buddhist religion in China. Confucianism also resurged due to the political attitudes of the people. Since Buddhism was the favored religion, it was also identified with the abuses of the rulers. Meanwhile, Confucianism, which was out of favor with the court, became the symbol of social reform. It is somewhat similar to the political process in the United States. When the Democrats have control of the Congress and the executive branch, the people, who had voted the Democrats into power, complain against the prevailing national policy and then look to the Republicans as the true representatives of the people. When the Republicans are in power, the reverse occurs. In other words, the grass is always greener on the other side. In this case, a violent reaction against Buddhism eventually erupted.

The first major persecution of Chinese Buddhists took place in about the tenth century. Toward the beginning of the Sung dynasty (960-1279), Neo-Confucianism displaced Buddhism at the royal court. Ironically Neo-Confucianism was similar to Buddhism, especially Ch'an (Zen), on many doctrinal points. Nevertheless, in 1019, the Emperor Chen-Tsung decreed that Buddhists and Taoists could possess the same rights as the Confucianists.

Centuries later the Mongols invaded China and easily conquered the weak Ming dynasty (1368-1644), and under them Buddhism enjoyed a second flowering. The Mongols treated all Chinese religions with respect, especially Buddhism, because they wanted to win over the Chinese people. They felt that the religious scholars had a strong influence, and if they could capture the loyalty of the intellectuals, the people would soon follow and accept them as Chinese royalty. They were generally successful for a time.

Thus Buddhism joined Confucianism and Taoism as a member of the religious family of China. Although Buddhism was an adopted child, the Chinese people came to regard Chinese Buddhism as one of their own. This religious structure was to last until Maoist communism put to ruins all religions in China.

Tibet

In the land some call Shangri-La, isolated by the towering Himalayan Mountains, hides the remote country of Tibet, where Buddhism has flourished in a form quite different from the original teachings of Gautama, the Buddha.

Tibet is mostly a tableland, called Chang Tang ("Northern plain"), and is the highest country in the world. The physical features of the Tibetans are not only distinct from their Indian and Chinese neighbors but as yet anthropologists have not determined their ethnic origins. Furthermore, there are many types of people who live in Tibet. After many centuries, it was not politics that united the Tibetans into one people but rather religion in the form of Lamaism—Tibetan Buddhism.

The earliest accounts of Buddhism in Tibet date back to the seventh century A.D., during which Songtsen Gampo unified Tibet into a single nation and became its first king in 625. Prior to this, Tibet was a land of separate tribes, and the prevailing belief was the ancient religion Boen, a mixture of shamanism, magic and primitive Nature worship. The Tibetans initially did not welcome Buddhism. Only after Buddhism had absorbed some of the occultic features of Boen did the Tibetans accept Tibetan Buddhism as their own.

Tibetan tradition states that Buddhism first came to Tibet while Lhato Thori was ruler; that one day a casket fell from the heavens and landed at his feet while he stood on the roof of his palace. Buddhist books and a model of a golden pagoda were in the casket, and within the books were written six syllables: *Om Mani Padme Hum,* which became a sacred prayer of the Tibetans. The translation of the syllables is "Hail to the Jewel in the Lotus," or simply "Hail to the Buddha in our Hearts." Tibetan Buddhists believe that the continuous chanting of these syllables will deliver a person from the cycle of rebirth and send that person to nirvana at death.

Historical records present a clearer understanding for the emergence of Buddhism in Tibet than in India or China. After Songtsen Gampo began his reign, he married a Nepalese princess and a Chinese princess, who were both devout Buddhists and who had tremendous influence over the king. Songtsen Gampo subsequently built Buddhist temples, sent Tibetan scholars and youth to surrounding countries to study Buddhism, and imported Buddhist teachers. Furthermore, he moved the capital from Yarlung to Lhasa ("God's place"), which became the center of Lamaism. His favor of Buddhism did much to convert many of his people to that religion.

Trisong Detsen succeeded Songtsen Gampo to the throne and his policies further secured Buddhism in Tibet. He instituted the first Buddhist monasteries in Tibet, and he continued to import Buddhist masters, one of whom was Padmasambhava who brought the doctrine of Tantric Buddhism from India. The Tibetans quickly adopted his teachings, and soon he became revered and honored in Tibet as the "Precious Teacher." The syncretism of the ancient religion of Boen (or Bon), the doctrines of Tibetan Buddhism and the Tantric practices of Padmasambhava developed into Tibetan

Lamaism, distinctly different from Theravada and Mahayana Buddhism. As a separate vehicle, it became known as Vajrayana Buddhism or the "Diamond Vehicle" of Buddhism.

"Tibetan Buddhism took on the particular form of Lamaism from the very vital role of the 'lama' or priest-teacher, around whom religious activity centered," writes Laura Pilarski in her valuable book on the religious history of Tibet. "Lamaism developed into a complex and intricate system, with its own philosophical dialectics and metaphysics, its different aspects of yoga, its numerous rituals, popular traditions, literature, and systems of divination."[12]

The *Kangyur*, some hundred volumes of text, are the sacred scriptures of Lamaism. Tibetan tradition states that the *Kangyur* are books composed of the direct teachings of the Buddha. The famous *Bardo Thodol*, the Tibetan Book of the Dead, is another significant Tibetan scripture. It reveals the soul's experiences during the forty-nine days between death and rebirth.

One son in every family was expected to join a monastery. Since Tibet has lacked a school system until modern times and since the monasteries were open to all, many Tibetans chose monkhood in order to receive an academic education or training in particular skills. This afforded Tibetans of the lower class to reach positions of respect as monks. Thus, it is understandable why one out of every six Tibetans joined a monastery so that by the twentieth century there were estimated to be 750,000 monks and nuns in Tibet.

Back in the eighth and ninth centuries, Tibet and China had clashed in a series of border wars. Finally, in 821 they signed a peace agreement which was carved on a stone pillar at Lhasa. Although the treaty brought peace with China, the internal affairs of Tibet were marked with blood. Lang Darma seized the throne and promptly initiated a severe persecution of the Buddhists by destroying temples and forcing Buddhist leaders to flee from Tibet. The following two centuries were a dark age for the Tibetan people and their new religion.

Finally, belief in Buddhism returned to Tibet with renewed vigor. The Buddhist revival is called the Tibetan Renaissance. It not only stabilized the country, but it also set up a new ruling power out of its own ranks of Lamaism.

Two outstanding figures lived during this period of revival. One was Pandit Atisha, a Buddhist scholar from Bengal who came to Tibet in about 1042. He founded the Kadampa sect, which later evolved into the Gelukpa order, the official sect of the Dalai Lamas. Also in the eleventh century lived a Tibetan saint often referred to as the St. Francis of Tibetan Buddhism. His name was Milarepa. He was called "Cotton-clad" because he wore only a cotton garment. A poet and an ascetic, his life is said to have exemplified compassion and renunciation.

In 1071, the Sakya order was established in Shigatse. This Tibetan school combined Tantric mysticism with the philosophy of Mahayana Buddhism. In this sect, monks were not required to be celibates. Thus a religious hierarchy was secured among certain families as the post of abbot was passed from father to son.

In the thirteenth century Godan, a descendant of Genghis Khan, invited the leader of the Sakya sect in Tibet to come to Mongolia to devise a writing system for the Mongols. The interaction between these two peoples had the twofold effect of implanting Tantric Buddhism within the Mongol dynasty and installing the Sakya sect in political power in Tibet. Later, Kublai Khan declared Lamaism the national religion of his empire and selected Phakpa, the leader of the Sakyas, as his spiritual advisor. Meanwhile the Sakyas gave full political authority to the grand Lama in Tibet by marrying church with state.

After the Ming dynasty in China overthrew the Mongol rule in Central Asia, the Chinese emperors extended the same patronage toward Tibet as the Mongols. As the Mongol dynasty collapsed, however, the power of the Sakyas also dwindled. Religious and economic corruption had plagued the Tibetan government under the Sakyas. The people clamored for reform. A brilliant scholar answered the call. Tsong Khapa preached for reform and unity. He founded the Ganden monastery, and his disciples became known as the Gelukpa or "those who follow the virtuous way."

One of the important reforms of Tsong Khapa was his decree prohibiting marriage among his followers. This policy terminated the transmitting of political and religious power from father to son. It also struck at the blatant immorality among monks and nuns who had glorified sexual union as a "tantric" experience. He instituted high academic standards in monasteries for any spiritual advancement. He did much to reform Tibetan Buddhism. Nevertheless, he still could not remove magic and occultism from it.

To the Tibetans yellow is a symbol of growth and purity. Tsong Khapa ordered his followers to wear yellow hats to distinguish their faith as pure and distinct from other Buddhist sects. The other Tibetan schools of Buddhism, particularly the Nyingmapa sect, wore red hats. Thus, the Nyingmapa, who take for their doctrinal base the teachings of Padmasambhava, are referred to as the "Red Hats," while the Gelukpa, who regard Tsong Khapa as their Church Father, are referred to as the "Yellow Hats."

As head and tulku of the Gelukpa sect,[13] Gedun Truppa

succeeded Tsong Khapa who had passed away in 1419. After Gedun Truppa died, the system of incarnations from Lama to Lama was instituted. The Tibetans believed that since Gedun Truppa had attained Buddhahood and therefore was liberated from rebirth, that he had chosen to transmigrate to another human body to reassume leadership over the Gelukpa.

In the seventeenth century, Sonam Gyatso, head of the Gelukpa and incarnation of Gedun Truppa, visited the court of Altan Khan in Mongolia. Altan Khan was converted. He soon proclaimed Tibetan Buddhism the national religion of Mongolia. He conferred the title of Dalai Lama on Sonam Gyatso. *Dalai* is a Mongolian word which means "ocean." Thus, the rendering of Dalai Lama is "ocean of wisdom." Although this title has gained universal acceptance, the Tibetans still call their leader Gyalwa Rimpoche, "the victorious one."

Yonten Gyatso, the grandson of Altan Khan, became the fourth Dalai Lama. Naturally the Mongols favored the Gelukpa, which in fact disturbed the Tsang dynasty who ruled over most of Tibet. Fearing the incursion of the Mongols, the Tsang rulers launched a merciless persecution of the Gelukpa, which ironically prompted the Mongols to invade Tibet and crush the Tsang army. The Mongol conquest of Tibet not only ended the persecution but terminated the existing political system. In 1642, Gushi Khan transferred control of Tibet to Ngawang Lobsang, the fifth Dalai Lama. The establishment of the Dalai Lama as the religious and political head of Tibet became complete.

Ngawang Lobsang Gyatso, as ruler of Tibet, ordered the construction of the Potala Palace, which has become a landmark to the country's national culture. It is entirely made out of stone and took about a half century to complete. It is to the Potala Palace that Tibetan Buddhists make their holy pilgrimage. The former teacher of Ngawang Lobsang was Panchen Rimpoche, "precious great sage." "Successors of Panchen Rimpoche became known in the world as Tashi Lamas."[14]

Although it did not become a part of China, from the eighteenth century Tibet was a protectorate of the Manchu dynasty in China for almost two centuries. During this period, the Dalai Lama was the titular head of Tibet. As China became a melon sliced by vying European powers, Tibet once again enjoyed self-rule. The British, however, conducted bloody, military expeditions into Tibet in an attempt to wrestle Tibet from China. Finally, after the 1911 revolution in China, the Dalai Lama negotiated a peace treaty with the British and declared the independence of Tibet.

From 1911 to 1950, Tibet experienced relative peace because of the protection of the British. Thubten Gyatso, the thirteenth Dalai Lama, guided Tibet for twenty-one of those years. Again corruption had become rampant within the religious and political systems of Tibet. Thubten Gyatso fought to reform both the church and the government. "The active reformer moved into many areas," states Laura Pilarski. "He revised scales of taxation to assess the rich more adequately; revamped the penal system, abolishing capital punishment and all severe sentences involving mutilation except for treason; and introducing a few school reforms."[15] In December 1933, Thubten Gyatso died, but not before warning his country that unless Tibetans learn to protect their land that it would soon be conquered. His words became a tragic prophecy.

Although Tibet emerged from the turmoil of World War 2 unscathed, the turbulent years of political instability within

Tibet starting in 1933 were a prelude to a civil war which began in 1947. Since the current candidate for the Dalai Lama was still a child and Tibet was led by a weak regency, Tibet lacked a forceful and a dynamic leader in a precarious time when Tibet had lost her protection from the south and when the Chinese Communists were routing the Nationalist government in China.[16]

Fearing an invasion from China, the Tibetans prepared to send "delegations to visit India, Nepal, Great Britain and the United States to seek official recognition of the country's independent status, along with some help in keeping out the Chinese. These delegations, however, never left Lhasa because of the negative response from the countries approached. No nation, not even India, wanted to push Tibetan claims against Chinese ones."[17] Finally, the Chinese Communists invaded Tibet on October 7, 1950.

On November 17, Tenzin Gyatso, at the age of fifteen, was installed as the fourteenth Dalai Lama. A month later he removed himself to the Sikkim border and out of personal danger so that, if the Chinese were successful in their military drive toward Lhasa, he could flee to India and thereby take "the heart of the people with him."[18] In May 1951, China annexed Tibet. The Dalai Lama then decided to return to Lhasa to comfort his people. The Chinese initially tried to convert the Tibetans through peaceful propaganda, but the Tibetans resented having their ancient customs disturbed by a new belief system.

Finally, in March 1959, in one of the most dramatic episodes of current history, the Dalai Lama fled his country when he realized that he could better serve his people outside of Tibet. Disguising himself in soldier's clothes,[19] joining the rest of his family who had taken different paths to the same point, traveling on yakskin rafts, crossing lofty mountains, treacherous rivers and valleys, the Dalai Lama reached the border of India safely after fifteen days of adventure.

Thousands of Tibetans have since left their country, which has been swallowed by Chinese communism, and have joined the Dalai Lama in exile. It is in him, however, that there is the hope that one day their culture, their country and their religion will be restored. "In him Tibet—past, present and future—existed."[20] And in him is still the symbol of Tibetan Buddhism.

Japan

The myths regarding the origin of the Japanese people are many and varied. One of the more interesting legends appeared in *National Geographic* (April 1978) in which Audrey Topping considered the possibility that the Chinese had colonized Japan.

Actually her article is on the history of the Ch'in dynasty, but in one digression she relates a story told by the historian Edward Thomas Williams. According to Williams, Ch'in Shih Huang Ti, a ruthless emperor during the Ch'in dynasty, commissioned a fleet of ships to embark upon a quest for an elixir whose contents would confer immortality. A captain of one of the ships returned to the emperor with valuable news. Captain Hsu reported that he had located the Immortals who dwelt on a large island and who possessed the elixir. The Immortals, however, would not part with it unless the emperor sent them the finest youth of China. The emperor, desiring more than anything else not to die, immediately had 3,000 of China's finest youth delivered to the Immortals. The captain set sail once again but never returned.

Topping adds a few more details to Williams's story, leaving the possibility open that the captain and the children might have colonized Japan.

However interesting this legend may be, the true origin of the Japanese people has remained a mystery. Although Japanese ancestry probably did not come from China, the Japanese have imported much from the Chinese throughout history. One import from China has had tremendous influence on the Japanese culture. It is, of course, Buddhism. Many of the different forms of Japanese Buddhism were born in China and grew into adulthood on the island where Captain Hsu might have settled.

The absorption of Buddhism into Japanese culture was far easier than into Chinese culture. The islands of Japan were often fertile in absorbing the arts, philosophy and theology which might be in season in China. After Buddhism had rooted itself in China, it naturally followed that the Japanese would plant it in their religious framework.

Buddhism did not have to contend with extremely hostile doctrines in Japan as it did in China (that is, Confucianism). Although Shinto initially opposed the new religions, it did not for long. Just how much of early Shinto in Japan was Chinese is unknown. Actually it was a name given to a variety of religions which consist of the beliefs and practices of both the native Japanese and the subsequent invading peoples.

Shinto means "way of the gods," and is derived from the Chinese *shen-tao*. John B. Noss points out: "Cultured Japanese in ancient times often borrowed Chinese words, as being more distinguished. In pure Japanese, the word is *Kami-no-michi*, which has the same meaning."[21]

Since Shinto lacked a systematic dogma of its own, Buddhism complemented it well. Shinto had been little more than the worship of ancestors and native divinities, particularly the sun goddess, Amaterasu, who has been honored at the Grand Imperial Shrine at Ise' until 1945. Shinto also claimed that the Japanese islands and people were special creations of the gods, a not too peculiar belief of any people.[22]

As happy as the marriage of Buddhism and Shinto has been, there have been times in history when they have spatted. In the seventeenth century, Shinto was restored as the authentic Japanese religion. In 1868, Emperor Mutsuhito declared Shinto the state religion under the title *Daikyo*, or "great doctrine." Within twenty years, however, the emperor renounced it, and in 1884 it lost its status.

Because Buddhism contributed new insights into human thought and conduct, the more liberal Japanese quickly accepted it when it first came to the islands. The imperial family subsequently adopted a form of Buddhism, and soon it spread first to the aristocracy and then to the common people.

After Buddhism spread from China down the Korean peninsula, one of three Korean kings, Syong-Myong, presented the emperor of Japan, Kimmei (540-71), with Buddhist scriptures and images of the historical Buddha in A.D. 552. This was the introduction of Buddhism to Japan.

The Japanese court received Buddhism with mixed emotions. Some feared that the native gods and goddesses might be angered; others welcomed it as a way for Japan to keep pace with other civilized nations in Asia. Finally each side agreed to a compromise: Buddhist worship was to be allowed temporarily as an experiment. A terrible pestilence swept through the house where the image of Buddha was kept. The Japanese received this as a sign of the wrath of the gods. They quickly denounced Buddhism and threw the image of Buddha into a canal.

Despite this first disastrous experience of Buddhism in Japan, Buddhist artifacts continued to filter to the islands. During the reign of Bidatsu (572-85), Buddhist worship was not merely allowed—his son became an ardent believer. Another plague ensued, and again a Buddhist temple was burned. The plague grew worse, however, and that convinced the Japanese court that the cause of the plague was the rejection rather than the acceptance of the Buddha. The Japanese subsequently accorded Buddhism awe and respect.[23]

Once Buddhism (specifically, Mahayana Buddhism) was accepted by the Japanese and established into the Japanese religious framework, it began to subdivide into a number of sects just as it had in China. In 784, the emperor moved the imperial court to Nagaoka from Nara. Ten years later, he transferred it to Heian, known today as Kyoto. The capital remained in Heian until 1868. It was called "the capital of peace and tranquility," or *Heian-kyo*.

During the Heian period (794-1185), the first major schools of Japanese Buddhism took hold.[24] They were the schools of Tendai and Shingon. Both are still alive in Japan.

Saicho (posthumously known as Dengyo daishi, 767-822) brought the first new Buddhist system into Japan. As a Buddhist monk, Saicho traveled to China to deepen his spiritual knowledge of the ancient religion. Exhausting his studies of the traditional Buddhist schools, he came across a new system called T'ien-T'ai in Chinese. He returned to Japan with this system which became known as Tendai in Japanese.

Fortunately Saicho had the favor of Emperor Kammu (782-805); otherwise his return might have been lost in obscurity. Interestingly, one of the reasons the emperor favored the

Tendai school was the location of Saicho's monastery, situated on Mount Hiei northeast of Heian. Ancient tradition had spread the belief that demons entered the capital from the northeast. With the building of the Tendai monastery, Heian was now protected from hostile spirits. The monastery (Enryakuji) soon was known as "the center for the protection of the nation."

Although the Japanese nobility and peasants accepted the Tendai school, leaders and adherents of the older, established scholastic schools intensely opposed it.[25] Finally, after Saicho's death, the Tendai school was accorded its place among the other sects of Japanese Buddhism.

The Tendai school taught that synthesis of meditation and moral purity result in discovering one's own Buddha nature. It was a school which incorporated "the various views on Truth which had been evolved during the course of time,"[26] including the belief that the nature of the Buddha was not limited to a specific historical being but is in all beings in the form of Dharmakaya.

In 816, Kukai (Kobo daishi, 774-835) founded the Shingon-shu, or the Shingon ("true word") school. He also studied in China and returned to Japan with a Buddhist sect which was born on the continent but developed on the islands. In China, the Shingon was known as Chen-yen.

The Shingon school stressed esoteric elements of Tantric Buddhism in its sacraments and rituals. It attracted many of the superstitious Japanese because of the magic and the occult in its rituals. Its spectacular ceremonies became very popular even with many Japanese who were not associated with the Shingon.

The early Heian period was a time of fervent interest in both the old and new schools of Buddhism. The late Heian period, however, was a time of religious disillusionment and moral deterioration. The emperors were weak; the clergy were materialistic; the people were dissolute. Civil discord and turmoil marked society in Japan. Religious corruption reached its height when monasteries hired mercenary armies to war with other monasteries, first in doctrinal disputes and then for power and wealth. Japan was in desperate need of reform and spiritual revival.

After the collapse of the Fujiwara power in the twelfth century, the leadership of Japan fell into the hands of the Minamoto clan. Although they continued to install emperors on the throne in Kyoto, the true ruler of Japan was the head of the Minamoto clan. He became known as the shogun and he lived in Kamakura. During the Kamakura period (1185-1336), the shogunate governed Japan with absolute power.

The rise of the samurai marked the feudal life of the Kamakura period in Japan. The warrior of the Kamakura period displaced the courtier of the Heian period as the epitome of Japanese ideals.[27] It was in the philosophy of the samurai class *bushi* that the key to the development of Buddhism was provided during this period in Japanese history. E. Dale Saunders elaborates:

> The decline of Heian society had been accompanied by the increasing corruption of a patronized clergy, more and more out of touch with the lower classes. All this, set against the background of disorder and confusion, contributed to emphasizing the idea of salvation for the warrior. He was not attracted to the Esoteric ceremonies of the Tendai and Shingon schools, with their beautiful but impersonal rites, nor by the coldly intellectual concepts of the older sects. The warrior insisted on the immediacy of salvation, and he favored the sect that could offer him

this. Salvation was no longer confined to the monasteries;
it was now to be sought on the battlefield as well.[28]
The Japanese, therefore, were ready for a Buddhist discipline
which emphasized a simple faith in the Buddha. The Amidist
schools answered this need. Genshin (942-1017) and Ryonin
(1071-1132) were forerunners of the Pure Land sects. They
advocated a worship of Amida, the Buddha who rules over
a "western paradise" or a Pure Land. Honen (1133-1212),
however, was the monk who many religious scholars consider the founder of Japanese Amidism.

In 1175, Honen established the Jodo sect (School of the
Pure Land). He taught a gentle and simple faith in the lord
Buddha (Amida). His life and teachings demonstrated this
kind of faith, and thus he gained a large following. He believed that the formula *Namu Amida Butsu* (or *Nembutsu*)
would assure salvation in this corrupt age and entry into
the Pure Land at death to those who uttered it from their lips
with sincere devotion and believed in their hearts. He taught
that faith in the compassion of Amida Buddha would bring
true happiness to the believers. Finally, Honen believed in
salvation by simple repetition of the *Nembutsu* only, although
good works reflected Buddha's compassion and mercy flow-
ing through the believer's life.

Honen received Shinran Shonin (1173-1262) as a disciple in
1201. Shonin was not only Honen's favorite pupil but he became Honen's most important follower, for Shinran founded
the Jodo-Shinshu ("true school of the pure land").

Shinran held that only by faith can a believer be saved. He
emphasized even less than Honen monasticism and even
more the worship of Amida. The faith which he preached was
for all the people. Whoever surrenders to the Buddha and
accepts him as savior would receive admission into paradise.

This was the Buddhist faith that the Japanese longed for.

During the Kamakura period, Myoan Eisai (1141-1215) was responsible for the introduction of Zen as an independent Buddhist sect to the Japanese, although Zen ideas had long since been in Japan. Because the established order vigorously opposed Eisai, he had to seek protection from the shogun, Minamoto Yoriie (1182-1204). He subsequently had to compromise with the shogun on matters of doctrine and practice. This was a principal reason for the interaction of ideas between Zen and the samurai philosophy.

In contrast to Eisai, Dogen (1200-53) refused to mix any other ideas or concepts with Zen. He taught that the attainment of Buddhahood is achieved through continuous effort at reaching deeper levels of awareness, and not a quick experience stimulated by a flash of understanding during meditation, as Eisai believed.

The origin of the word *zen* is from the Sanskrit word *dhyana*, which means "meditation." *Dhyana* evolved into *ch'an* in Chinese and into *zen* in Japanese. Although Zen Buddhism is believed to have been born in China in the sixth century, it is in Japan that Zen has developed into the sophistication it enjoys today. Zen came to Japan in about the ninth century, but it was not until the thirteenth century that Zen became popular.

Most forms of Zen Buddhism train their acolytes (followers) with mental exercises to deepen spiritual concentration and to teach that ultimate truth cannot be understood until the meditator reaches inner Enlightenment. Words are futile to express Ultimate Truth. Thus *koans*, irrational phrases or stories, are used to cut through intellectual barriers and raise the mind to illumination. A famous example is the Hakuin *koan:* "What is the sound of one hand clapping?"[29]

E. Dale Saunders comments:

Like Amidism, Zen aims to bring salvation into the ken of the common man. While Amidism stressed salvation through other, i.e., through the Buddha Amida, Zen emphasizes salvation within oneself. Every man has the Buddha-nature, and this nature is perceptible through a "realization of self." Hence Zen more than any other sect stresses the qualities of self-understanding and self-reliance as prerequisites for apprehending one's own nature.[30]

In the thirteenth century, the reformer Nichiren (1222-82) taught a doctrine which differed considerably in temperament with the Amidist and Zen schools. Furthermore, he denounced Honen and other religious leaders whom he felt had drifted away from the doctrines of Saicho. He believed that it was "the duty of the government to see that they [heretics] are put to death."[31]

Because of his vocal attacks against the government and all forms of Buddhism outside of Tendai, he was exiled in 1261 to Izu where he became further convinced that he alone taught the true path to Buddhahood and that only he possessed the answers needed for Japan to lift herself from spiritual decadence. Although he was soon released from Izu, he continued to voice his thoughts publicly. He was subsequently sentenced to death. The execution, however, never occurred. Instead, he was removed to a hermitage at Ikegami where he passed away.

Whereas other Japanese sects practiced tolerance to some extent, Nichiren's followers were fanatic in their beliefs and exclusive in their practice which drifted toward Tantrism. Nichiren taught that the efficacy of chanting "*Namu-myoho-renge-kyo*" ("reverence to the Wonderful Law of the Lotus") coupled with a zealous life dedicated to the principles of the Buddha result in salvation.

Nichiren Buddhism was and still is an ultranationalistic religion. In a feudal period when warriors reflected the spiritual attitudes of their society, nationalistic sects (such as the Amidist and Zen schools) naturally arose in the Kamakura period. Yet none of them epitomized the nationalism of a Japanese religion more than Nichirenism.

After the Kamakura period, Japanese Buddhism formed no new schools equal in significance to the previous schools mentioned. In the Tokugawa period (1600-1868), only Hakuin of the Rinzai Zen sect presented new, exceptional insights into Buddhism.[32] During this time, Japan experienced relative calm after the turbulence of the preceding period. Henceforth Buddhism continued to exist as a traditional, formal institution which remained for centuries primarily apathetic.

In 1867, the shogunate fell and the Meiji period (1868-1912) began. This was an era when Japan became increasingly exposed to western technology and thought. Buddhism, the symbol of the establishment, became an obvious target for many of the progressive Japanese. As the Japanese welcomed the creation of a new order, Buddhism suffered a short period of discrimination. The consequence of this action was that Buddhism was awakened from its passivity. It began to adjust to twentieth-century Japan and to meet the challenge of Christianity.

FIVE

Contemporary Buddhist Movements

AS THE VARIOUS FORMS of Buddhism have arrived in the United States, there has been a general desire among these schools to achieve some type of unity. But, just as the leaves of a maple have their source in a tree and yet must inevitably fall and go their own way because of their individuality, so the individual Buddhist schools divide and separate because of their difference in practice and doctrine despite their common origin. And so, the Eastern winds are blowing across the West and bringing with them foliage of a variety of shapes, colors and designs, and all from the same tree.

Theravada Buddhism

Having encountered so many forms of Buddhism, I have often wondered, What was the original form of Buddhism when Gautama, the Buddha, held sway over a community of monks and nuns in India twenty-five centuries ago? To reach back into time and experience the daily life of a follower of Gautama is, of course, not possible. Equally impossible would be to discover that school of Buddhism with that religious philosophy and practice which is the identical twin of the sangha of Gautama's day. Even if that Buddhist school existed, how would we know that it is like Gautama's sangha or, more importantly, how could we come to a consensus that it is? And so, my thoughts can only drift in that realm between speculation and imagination.

Theravada Buddhism might be a key in understanding what Buddhism was like during its early days, however, since Theravada Buddhism has tried to maintain the essence of the teachings of the Buddha without indulging upon further revelations. The simplicity and the fundamentalism of Theravada Buddhism might be the clearest image of a scene now long past.

Theravada Buddhism can best be found in Burma, Thailand, Cambodia, Laos and particularly Sri Lanka (formerly Ceylon), where it is referred to as the "Old Wisdom School." Yet, even in Indochina, Theravada Buddhism has experienced a history of ups and downs. It was highly popular during the immediate centuries following the birth of Buddhism. About the fifth century A.D., it began to decline and for fifteen centuries it slowly withered.

The nineteenth century was the turning point for Theravada Buddhism. First, the faith of the Buddhists was revived in reaction to the challenge the Christian missionaries who brought in their new religion. Second, profound thinkers emerged to defend the ancient religion. Third, the translation of the Pali texts into Western languages gave it strength to spread beyond its Asian borders.

At first Theravada Buddhism struggled weakly against the evangelism of the Christian faith in Indochina during the nineteenth century. In Ceylon, however, the Christian movement did not go unchallenged. Four men rose up to turn back the tide. Two were Easterners and two were Westerners.

Mohotiwatte Gunananda was a Ceylonese monk who studied both the Christian Scriptures and western rationalist writings which were critical of Christianity. From his research, he formed arguments which he used to preach against the Christian faith. From 1866 to 1873, he publicly debated with Christian missionaries. These debates were published and distributed throughout Indochina and the West.

Henry S. Olcott, an American, read these transcripts and was impressed with Gunananda's arguments. In 1875, Olcott and Madame Blavatsky organized the Theosophical Society which has some of its roots in Olcott's understanding of Theravada Buddhism. Five years later, he established the Buddhist Theosophical Society which has been responsible for building numerous Buddhist schools in Sri Lanka. The efforts of Olcott were chief reasons why the country is the center for the Theravada missionary movement.

Olcott needed an interpreter to communicate in Ceylonese. His interpreter was Anagarika Dharmapala, one of the most dynamic thinkers of the Theravada tradition. It was Dharmapala who organized the Maha Bodhi Society in 1891, which has branches throughout the world. And it was

Dharmapala who was primarily responsible for stimulating interest in Theravada Buddhism in the West through his speeches and writings.

The spread of Theravada Buddhism would have gone nowhere, however, if it had not been for T. W. Rhys Davids who founded the Pali Text Society in 1881. It was the work of this society which bore fruit in the translation of much of the Pali Canon into English. The English translations, in turn, stimulated wide interest in Theravada Buddhism starting in England and rippling out to all parts of Europe.

Although Theravada Buddhism has been more popular in England and Europe than Mahayana Buddhism up until the middle of the twentieth century, it has had little success in the United States. Small centers have cropped up here and there but few Americans have committed themselves to Theravada Buddhism.

In the United States, most Indochinese immigrants are Theravada Buddhists in name only, for few hold to the religious practices of their belief. In the late 1970s, however, with the advent of the Vietnamese boat people, Theravada Buddhism has taken deeper root in our society. Time will tell if it will bear fruit in this country as have other forms of Buddhism.

Chinese Buddhism

In June 1978, the Himalayan International Institute sponsored the International Congress on Yoga, Meditation and Holistic Health in Chicago. I was able to attend a seminar where I saw an interesting presentation on Tai Chi. The demonstrator was Al Chung-liang Huang. Huang had grown up in China where he received his training in the martial arts, particularly in Tai Chi. Currently, he is the director of the

Lan T'ing Institute in Sausalito, California.

As a youngster, I had thought of the martial arts as merely techniques by which men and boys could demonstrate their machismo. Frequent visits to Bruce Lee and other Kung Fu movies helped reinforce this idea in my mind. After listening to Al Huang, however, I realized that the spiritual foundation of the martial arts is much more significant than I had considered before.

Tai Chi may not be as well known as Judo and Kung Fu, yet within Caucasian religious circles of Eastern philosophy in the United States, Tai Chi is the most respected and practiced of the martial art techniques. It combines grace and beauty with a highly developed system of thought which is almost as alluring as Zen to those Westerners who are seeking a new religion centered on meditation.

If we observe the new religious trends in our society, we can see other Chinese influences which have a spiritual base besides Tai Chi. In the field of health, acupuncture is becoming increasingly acceptable. For both the mystics and the superstitious, the Taoist practice of throwing coins is becoming more popular. And, of course, the *I Ching* is now a standard work in most libraries and bookstores.

While Chinese Buddhism may be finding a new home in the United States, in its homeland it is being cast out. Despite Communist claims that they allow religious freedom in mainland China, the Communist government has in the past aimed to systematically liquidate all forms of religion. The Chinese Buddhist Association was established in 1953 to do just that to Buddhism. The role of the CBA obviously has been to convert Buddhists into Maoist Communists. Most temples have been abandoned, and only a small number of Buddhists attend those which are open. Perhaps the "Modernization policies of Deng Xiaoping, the current leader of the People's Republic of China, will end suppression of religious expression. Time will tell.

Meanwhile there is a strong number of Chinese Buddhists in Taiwan and Hong Kong. After Mao Tse-tung took over mainland China, the Buddhist Association of the Republic of China was organized in Taiwan in 1952. Most of these Buddhists belong to the Ching T'u ("pure land") school of Buddhism. This school (like its Japanese cousins, the Amidist schools) teaches salvation by faith and was sown among the common people.

Chinese-Americans are not as devoted to a single school of Buddhism as their Chinese brothers and sisters or as the Japanese-Americans. Buddhist temples in the "Chinatown" sections of large cities are often a syncretism of Buddhism, Confucianism, Taoism and folk religion. Furthermore, Chinese Buddhist churches usually operate as a secular organization rather than as a religious institution. They sponsor social activities for secular purposes and they function as a center through which Chinese-Americans can communicate and fellowship with each other.

In the late 1840s, Chinese began to immigrate to the United States. Because the American establishment rejected them, they clustered into isolated areas and started small businesses. These areas soon became known as "Chinatowns."

The Chinese brought to America all their native beliefs, and initially they worshiped in their homes. In the 1850s, they built their first temple, which was located in San Francisco. Kuan Kung, a Chinese martial hero, was worshiped as the principal deity of this temple.

As the older generations of Chinese-Americans pass away, so do the syncretistic Chinese temples. Many Chinese-

Americans now prefer their old folk religions over Buddhism and Taoism. Their New Year celebrations with dragons and parades are evidence of this preference.

Caucasians, meanwhile, are attracted to some schools of Chinese Buddhism such as Ch'an and T'ien-T'ai. The popularity of Zen Buddhism naturally has had a favorable effect on the spread of Ch'an among Caucasians because Zen derives from Ch'an. Hsuan Hua is probably the most popular Ch'an master in America today. He came from Hong Kong in 1959. Many Caucasians belong to his Sino-American Buddhist Association and Gold Mountain Dhyana Monastery. It seems that most Caucasians involved in Chinese Buddhism are attracted to the Chinese schools of Buddhism which offer meditation and monasticism.

Jodo Shinshu

Each July my father mans one of the booths at the Obon Festival and Bazaar in San Jose, California. I usually attend the festival. In my younger days, I would go to play bingo, toss coins at the different booths and partake of the delicious Japanese foods. Now I go only to see men, women and children dance in their colorful kimonos to traditional Japanese music. To see over one hundred dancers gracefully move in a circle, carefully opening and closing their fans in time with their hand and facial gestures, is an enriching experience for me.

The Obon, or "Festival of Joy," is a two-day event which takes place at Jodo Shinshu Buddhist churches throughout the United States. Obon, or Bon, is an abbreviation for Urabon, which means, "being hung upside down." It is both a time of celebration and a solemn religious occasion for Japanese Buddhists.

It is interesting to note how the Buddhists raise their money at these festivals. Bingo, raffle tickets, game booths—these are all ideas which Catholic and Protestant organizations have employed. Moreover, Western Christianity has influenced the Japanese Buddhists in America in other ways. Instead of calling their buildings temples, they call them churches. As a matter of fact, outward and sometimes inward appearances resemble simple Christian churches. A notable exception is the San Jose Buddhist Church whose architecture and gardens are exquisitely Japanese.

Jodo Shinshu Buddhists in America also have services on Sundays, again following the Christian custom, and their Sunday schools are modeled after Sunday schools of Protestant churches. Furthermore, Sunday services include sermons. The historical Buddha certainly preached many times, but this practice had been absent until modern times. In Japan a person goes to the temple whenever he or she desires, for every day is considered holy. The day and the frequency is entirely up to the individual.

As Western, and perhaps Christian, as it may seem on the outside, Jodo Shinshu Buddhism in America is still unmistakably Buddhist in its devotion to the Buddha and the Dharma, and specifically Amidist in its reverence to Honen and Shinran. Followers place their faith not in the Christian Creator but in Amida Buddha. They have no crosses but have Buddhist icons in the altars of their churches. They pray not in the name of Jesus Christ but invoke the *nembutsu*, *"Namu Amida Butsu"* ("Hail to the Buddha of eternal light and infinite life"). They believe that only by the grace and compassion of Amida Buddha will they be saved and be reborn in a "pure land" or "Western paradise," where Amida Buddha presides and where they will finally attain nirvana.

Jodo Shinshu Buddhists are not forced to make extreme sacrifices; they are not commanded to become scholars of their philosophy; they are not pressured into spending long hours in meditation. Understandably the Jodo Shinshu school is considered "the easy way," and even more understandably it is currently the most popular traditional Buddhist school in Japan.

But it has not always been so popular. Jodo Shinshu ("the true school of the pure land") was established when Shinran Shonin (1173-1262) completed the principle text of *Kyo Gyo Shin Sho* in 1224. Shinran, as well as Honen (the founder of Jodo Shinshu Buddhism), were severely persecuted. Only after Honen's death did the Amidist schools become acceptable.

Through the centuries the Amidist schools, particularly Jodo Shinshu, became very popular with the common people. During the late nineteenth century, when the Japanese began to immigrate to the United States, it was the commoner, the Jodo Shinshu Buddhist, who usually came. That is why most Japanese-Americans have some link with this school of Buddhism.

Nisaburo Hirano, a Japanese immigrant, established the first official Jodo Shinshu mission in San Francisco in 1899. Later this mission separated from its parent organization in Japan and it became the Buddhist Church of America, which currently has independent and branch churches throughout the United States. Nevertheless, although it receives no support from Japan, it is obliged to contribute financially to the home temples, Hompa Hongwanji and Nishi Hongwanji.

Until recently candidates for the ministry had to complete their theological training in Kyoto, Japan. Therefore they had to speak Japanese. Now they have a seminary in Berkeley, California, and their ministers are better able to communicate to the younger generations. From the close of World War 2 to the early seventies, the number of both clergy and laity has doubled so that now there are about 50,000 members.

Meanwhile, there are still many changes which are occurring in the Buddhist churches. Emma McCloy Layman, a noted psychology professor and expert on Buddhism, lists three changes in her book *Buddhism in America*. A headquarters staff member mentioned them to her: "(1) because members now have other social outlets, the church is becoming less of a community center or social activity center; (2) the church is becoming more ecumenical; and (3) rituals are becoming simplified."[1]

It is yet to be seen how these changes will affect the Jodo Shinshu churches, and whether these changes will secure the hearts and the minds of Japanese-Americans as they continue to integrate into Western society in their marriages and in their vocations.

The extent to which a Buddhist family is committed to their religion is the extent to which they show their devotion at their *Butsu-dan*. If they do not have one, then that could be a significant sign. If they do have one, then the depth of their faith will be exhibited there.

Butsu-dan is a Japanese term for the Buddhist altar. It literally means "a raised place for the Buddha." The *Butsu-dan* is a symbol of the world of the Buddha, and it is the sacred place for the living Buddha. The *Butsu-dan* was formerly anywhere the image of the Buddha was enshrined. Today, the family shrine is normally considered the *Butsu-dan*. The family shrine (or, the Buddha-shelf) is placed at the center of the home so that the Buddha can purify the daily life of the family.

There are three kinds of images of the Buddha in Jodo

Shinshu Buddhism. The first two are pictures and sculptures of the Buddha. Kakunyo Shoni (the third patriarch of the Hongwanji Temple) said, "In order to worship and express our reverence to the Buddha, we enshrine the statue or picture of the Buddha" (*Gaija-sho*). The third image is the seven-syllable, holy name (*Namu Amida Butsu*).

Images of the Buddha did not appear until long after his death because his disciples considered the worship of images of the Buddha a debasement of his dignity and holiness. Instead they used the ashes, hair, canes, clothes and other relics of the Buddha as objects of worship. As the centuries passed, image worship became divorced from idol worship, which the Buddhists of the Amidist schools forbid. They defined idol worship as worship of an object as the deity itself, but they defined image worship as worship of the deity through the use of an image. The image of the Buddha can be compared to the photograph of a loved one. You may have a photo of a loved one, and the picture will remind you of your loved one and foster affection, but you do not love the photograph itself.

Thus, images of the Buddha are placed in the *Butsu-dan* with pictures of deceased family members. Buddhists do not worship their loved ones at the *Butsu-dan* but they do gratefully thank them for what they have done for them, such as giving them life. Together with their loved ones, the Buddhists feel one with the Buddha and worship him as the source of all life.

As I described in chapter one, there are other articles at the *Butsu-dan*—rice, candles, incense, flowers, fruit and water. Rice is the sustenance of the Asian people; it represents life. Candles symbolize Enlightenment and the burning of incense symbolizes the act of purification. Flowers express impermanence and the compassion of the Buddha. They also represent the fulfillment of Enlightenment. Flowers with thorns, bad fragrance or bitter taste are forbidden, as is the rose of Sharon. Offerings are given at the *Butsu-dan* not to earn one's salvation but as an expression of gratitude to the Buddha.

Nichiren Shoshu

While I was in Japan recently, I had the good fortune to view a Japanese movie which portrayed the life of Nichiren Shonin. What fascinated me about this celluloid presentation of one of Japan's most controversial religious figures was not only the film itself but also the emotional response of the viewers. To me, their experience in this Japanese theater was similar to the experience of many Christians in Western theaters as they watch *The King of Kings* or *The Greatest Story Ever Told*.

The film depicted Nichiren as a highly religious, deeply spiritual man of principle, a man constantly persecuted and ostracized, a man sensitive to the needs of his followers and uncompromising in his beliefs, a man who spoke boldly against institutional hypocrisy and injustice, a man who was divinely called and miraculously delivered from death. Here was a man who was portrayed with many of the characteristics of Jesus. And the audience, who were mostly followers of Nichiren, either sat in awe or bowed their heads and wept. Here was a people whose love and devotion for this man were deep and sincere.

Those who have had a long heritage in the religion of Nichiren are some of the most religious and devout believers in Japan. They frequent the Minobusan Kuon-ji, the Grand Head Temple, which is located in a mountain retreat in the province of Kai and where also is located the mausoleum of Nichiren. They are attentive to their shrines and *Butsu-dans,* which they pass down from eldest son to eldest son. And they are devoted to the teachings of the Lotus Sutra. As faithful as they are, however, there are fewer people who are members of the orthodox sects of Nichiren Buddhism than of the other Japanese schools of Buddhism. Rather, most Nichiren Buddhists belong to the new sects, such as Reiyukai, Rissho Koseikai and particularly Soka Gakkai.

The Reiyukai was founded in 1925. It stresses the importance of ancestor worship. Rissho Koseikai was formed thirteen years later as an offshoot of Reiyukai. Acolytes not only seek Buddhahood but also are concerned for society. Soka Gakkai, however, is the sect with the largest following of Nichiren in Japan and is actually a lay movement to support and propagate Nichiren Shoshu, the "true Nichiren school."

Tsunesaburo Makiguchi and Josei Toda organized the Soka Kyoiku Gakkai (Value Creation Education Society) on November 8, 1930. Seven years later they formally established it. Makiguchi and Toda were successive presidents. After Toda died in 1958, Daisaku Ikeda became the third president in 1960. It has been during Ikeda's leadership that the Soka Gakkai has grown enormously.

In Japan, the Soka Gakkai has emphasized family conversions. Every follower is compelled to convert the rest of his family into the movement. Indoctrination is structured for the family, and organizational units are divided into family units. This has been very successful in converting Japanese families because the Japanese are strongly family oriented.

The Soka Gakkai is blatantly intolerant of other religious

groups, which is uncharacteristic of most Buddhist schools. Furthermore, there is an intense rivalry among the various nine Nichiren sects, with most of the Nichiren sects and the Soka Gakkai constantly at odds. The Soka Gakkai regards itself as the only true vehicle of Buddhism.

The current doctrines of the Soka Gakkai are the teachings of Nichiren and Toda, with Ikeda as the interpreter of the teachings. Makiguchi's teachings have been generally ignored.

The Komeito (Clean Government Party) was at one time the political arm of the Soka Gakkai but has since become independent of its mother organization. Nevertheless, most members of the Komeito are still members of the Soka Gakkai. And, at times, the Komeito has been the third most powerful party in the Diet (Japanese Parliament).

In 1960, Daisaku Ikeda started chapters of the Soka Gakkai in Southern California and South America. In California, the chapter was first called the Nichiren Shoshu Soka Gakkai, but later it became the Nichiren Shoshu Academy. Initially, the members were Japanese-Americans. In 1967, however, the Soka Gakkai began attracting Caucasians so that currently most members in America are now Caucasians.

Although both the Soka Gakkai in Japan and the Nichiren Shoshu Academy in America are both responsible to the head temple at Taisekiji near Fujiyama and to President Ikeda, the American organization has drifted away from its parent organization. Thus, the American branch is normally referred to as Nichiren Shoshu (the True Sect of Nichiren) rather than as Soka Gakkai.

One reason for this drift is that the Soka Gakkai in Japan has been extremely nationalistic and deeply involved in Japanese politics. But the Nichiren Shoshu Academy has merely instructed its members to consider what is beneficial to the United States. Nevertheless, there are strong emphases common to both groups. Emma Layman states: "Nichiren Shoshu in America, like its Japanese counterpart but unlike other Buddhist groups, is hostile toward other religions and sects, which it regards as 'heretical.' In a country with a dominant Judeo-Christian tradition, . . . opposition to Judaism and Christianity is played down in dealing with families of American converts, and emphasis is placed on the positive values of chanting."[2]

The Nichiren Shoshu also emphasizes closeness among its members. Discussion groups are a high priority along with the stress on family conversions. This close unity is a major reason why the Nichiren Shoshu has grown in the United States from 30,000 in 1965 to over 200,000 in 1974.

The *Saddharma Pundarika* ("the Sutra of the Lotus of the true law") or, simply, the Lotus Sutra is the holy scripture of the Nichiren Shoshu, and the invocation *"Namu-myoho-renge-kyo"* is an essential chant for salvation. In English, the invocation or *daimoku* is "Hail to the Lotus Sutra of the Mystical Law."

The *daimoku* is chanted before the *gohonzon,* a small altar which holds a mandala or a piece of paper which contains the invocation and the names of Nichiren and other holy personages. Members of the Nichiren Shoshu worship only at the *gohonzon.* The regular practice of chanting the *daimoku* will fulfill desires and thereby produce happiness, say members of Nichiren Shoshu. They are quick to note, however, that *"Namu-myoho-renge-kyo"* is the essence of all life. Therefore the true goal of their meditation is to become one with the cosmic universe, thus allowing the object of their desires to flow naturally to themselves.

Tantric Buddhism

On October 18, 1979, I saw and heard the Dalai Lama speak at Trinity Church in Boston. Trinity Church is famous for its New England architecture and Episcopalian decor, but I had come not to visit the church but to listen to the words of the spiritual leader of Tibetan Buddhism. I am sure that was why each person sat or stood in that church.

I felt a warmth and openness from this man who stood at the podium before an array of yellow, white and orange chrysanthemums. He was dressed in a traditional, Tibetan, red robe. And as he spoke, at first slowly in English and later through a translator, he systematically presented the major tenets of Mahayana Buddhism which gave me a clearer understanding of the philosophy of that religion. Although he dwelt mostly on Buddhist principles, his message was universal. He adjured cooperation among peoples of different nations and religions, stating that fundamental to all religions is compassion and kindness and that, when each person finds inner peace in his or her faith, then the world can experience outward peace.

The Dalai Lama was on the last stop of his twenty-two-city tour throughout the United States, which he had begun at an interfaith service at St. Patrick's Cathedral in New York. It was his first visit to this country. "He has been trying to visit the U.S. for six years," wrote *Time* magazine, "but the State Department has always discouraged the trip"[3] for fear that his visit might endanger their delicate negotiations with Peking. Chinese officials, however, have relaxed toward the Dalai Lama, even to the extent of wooing him to return to Tibet out of his twenty-year exile in Dhamsala, India.

American Buddhists will cherish for years the appearance in this country of the fourteenth Dalai Lama, whom many believe is the reincarnation of Chenrezi, a Bodhisattva and the patron deity of Tibet. Tantric Buddhists naturally used this occasion to publicize their activities and lectures which are regularly held throughout the United States. How much of an impact the Dalai Lama had during his six-week tour is yet to be seen.

"The Tantric tradition in America," says Emma Layman, "is expressed in three modes of practice—that of Tibetan and Mongolian Buddhism (sometimes called 'Lamaism'), the practice of the Japanese Shingon sect, and the mountain practice of the Shugendo of Japan. Of these, the Tantrism of Tibet is the only one which has had any substantial impact in America."[4]

Chogyam Trungpa Tulku and Tarthang Tulku are the best-known and most influential Tibetan masters in the United States today. Both are accorded the title Rinpoche, which means "precious master," and both fled Tibet after the Chinese invasion.

Chogyam Trungpa was born in northeastern Tibet in 1939. Like most Tibetans, his family was poor. At the age of one, however, he was taken from his poverty and was recognized to be the reincarnation of the tenth Trungpa Tulku. During his childhood, Kagyupa monks trained him in Tibetan Buddhism until he fled from Tibet in 1959.

During his exile, Chogyam Trungpa studied at Oxford University. In 1967, he founded the Samye-Ling Meditation Center in Scotland. Later he was involved in an automobile accident, soon after which he abandoned his Tibetan robes and began to dress in Western clothes. He married a young Englishwoman, which caused many difficulties in the Samye-Ling community.

The next stop of his exile was the United States. In 1970,

he established the Tail of the Tiger Community in the Green Mountains of Vermont. A year later he started his well-known Karma Dzong Meditation Center in Boulder, Colorado, where he currently resides.

Trungpa's constant theme is that he is a friend to his students and not a guru. He believes teachers should not force their egos upon students. Thus, his instruction is usually individual and personal. To most, he teaches a simple meditation which has little to do with mantras and mudras. To his advanced students, he teaches the traditional Tibetan meditational techniques. "In explaining Buddhist meditation," says Layman, "Chogyam Trungpa states first that it differs from the meditation of Christianity . . . in not involving a concept of some 'higher being' with which one tries to communicate. Rather, since there is no belief in a higher outside power in Buddhism, there is no seeking for something higher, but rather seeking to see what is."[5]

In contrast to the humble beginning of Chogyam Trungpa, Tarthang Tulku was born to the royal family of Gellek in eastern Tibet. He is regarded as one of the thirty reincarnated Lamas of the Tarthang Monastery. Monks of every sect of Tibetan Buddhism have played a role in his training. Before the Chinese invaded Tibet, he had become an abbot of a Nyingmapa monastery. In 1959, he also escaped the Chinese.

The first stop of his exile was Sikkim. In 1962, the Dalai Lama commissioned him to teach at Sanskrit University in Benares, India, because he was skilled in the Tibetan, Sanskrit, Pali, Hindi and English languages.

Finally, in 1968, he came to the United States where a year later he established the Tibetan Nyingmapa Meditation Center in Berkeley, California. This center was the first of its kind specifically to train Americans. In 1973, he founded the Nyingma Institute, also located in Berkeley where he lives with his wife and four children. The Nyingma Institute offers a degree program as well as courses in philosophy, art, language, and meditational theory and practice.

In 1975, Tarthang Tulku received nine hundred wooded acres in Sonoma County of northern California. He is currently building a country monastery which he has named Odiyan Tibetan Nyingma Cultural Center, a place of retreat for Tibetans and Americans alike. Odiyan is a name taken from the Indian city where supposedly Padmasambhava was born. It is the first Buddhist monastery to be designed in the traditional Tibetan style in America.

Tarthang Tulku tries to maintain a close relationship with all of his disciples, and in turn they regard him as their spiritual guide and teacher, a Buddhist master who is bringing the culture and the religion of Tibet to the West. In his instruction, he teaches both the exoteric and the esoteric teachings and practices of Tantric Buddhism.

A striking difference between the philosophies of Chogyam Trungpa and Tarthang Tulku is their positions on Tibetan culture. Chogyam Trungpa said in his popular book *Cutting through Spiritual Materialism* that the effort to appear Tibetan or to practice a Tibetan lifestyle is a hindrance to spiritual development. On the other hand Tarthang Tulku encourages his students to develop an appreciation for the Tibetan culture and has himself done much to preserve the literature, the art and the religion of Tibet.

Another form of Tantric Buddhism to come to North America is the Japanese school known as Shingon. It established the Koyasan Buddhist temple in Los Angeles in 1912. It has a tiny following in this country and most are of Japanese descent.

The third form of Tantric Buddhism and another Japanese school is the Shugendo, which means "way of spiritual power." The followers of the Shugendo are known as Yama-bushi, "ones who lie down or sleep in the mountains." They practice magic and asceticism primarily in the mountains.

Dr. Neville Warwick organized the Kailas Shugendo in North America. It is an offspring of the Yamabushi tradition, and as yet it has not enjoyed a wide following. Most of his disciples are Caucasians who refer to him as Ajari, a title given to those who have studied certain ascetic practices. The followers of Warwick wear blue-and-white checkered robes, and they are mostly known for their fire walk. The Kailas Shugendo is also under the spiritual tutelage of Lama Anagarika Govinda.

Lama Anagarika Govinda is actually a Tibetan Buddhist. He was a Westerner who had studied Islam, Christianity and Buddhism in a quest for "the true religion." In his own words, he says, "At the outset of my study I had felt more or less convinced of the superiority of Christianity (though not of the Christian Church), but the further I proceeded the more I found myself in agreement with Buddhism, until it became clear to me that Buddhism was the only religion I could follow with the fullest conviction."[6]

Whether many Westerners will travel the same spiritual odyssey as Govinda is difficult to discern. It would be im-possible to travel to Communist-held Tibet today, as he did several years ago. With such opportunities as seeing and hearing the Dalai Lama in this country, however, many Americans may take the first step. Meanwhile, Tibetan Bud-dhism, or Tantric Buddhism in general, is certainly not as popular as Zen, perhaps because it is "too exotic." Probably the difference is due more to a lack of qualified teachers, and to the fact that those who are accomplished in Tibetan Buddhism are either engaged in university work or are limited because of lack of funds.

In one respect the Communist invasion of Tibet has had a bright side for Tantric Buddhism. No doubt the Tibetan Buddhists would never have left their isolation in the Himalayas on their own. The forced exile of so many Lamas could possibly bring another tributary into the mainstream of American religions.

"A few years ago," says John Blofeld, "tragedy struck Tibet sending its people fleeing in thousands across the frontiers. Since then, the Lamas have come to recognize that, unless their homeland is recovered within a generation, the sacred knowledge may decline and vanish. Hence they are eager to instruct all who sincerely desire to learn. In this one respect, Tibet's tragic fate has been the world's gain."[7]

The Tibetans see another reason, a more important reason for looking at the bright side of their situation. The Dalai Lama expressed it this way: "Buddhism teaches us to respect our enemy. The enemy is the greatest guru, because, you see, your enemy teaches you patience. Your friend does not. Because of Chairman Mao's action I have had, as a refugee with many problems and difficulties, the opportunity to develop compassion and inner strength. This is a great thing."[8]

This was the same message he gave at Trinity Church in Boston.

Zen Buddhism
Furu-ike ya
Kawazu tobi-komu
Mizu no oto
This haiku is the most famous poem in Japan. Basho (1644-

94), whose family was Samurai but who became a wandering poet, composed this poem. He was also a devout Zen Buddhist and to many this poem reflects the essence of Zen. R. H. Blyth provides a unique translation:

The old pond.

A frog jumps in.

Plop![9]

While I was in Tokyo, I stayed with a Japanese family. One evening several friends of the family came to visit. Part of the evening was spent discussing the meaning of Basho's haiku. Different interpretations were offered—each with deliberate seriousness. Finally the host asked me what the poem meant to me. "No! No!" he exclaimed, after he heard my explanation. "You are being too intellectual and Western in your interpretation. Remember—this is a Japanese poem. It is the essence of Japanese. It is about an old pond and all is quiet. Suddenly a frog... Japan!"

Everyone laughed.

Humorous books with at least as many interpretations have been written on this poem. One typical modern interpretation is that it is only what it describes. One traditional view expresses the "quiet" motif. No matter; each individual will have his or her own thoughts and feelings in response to it.

To the Zen Buddhists this poem, and haiku in general, mirrors the true nature of Zen. Says D. T. Suzuki, "Zen naturally finds its readiest expression in poetry rather than in philosophy because it has more affinity with feeling than with intellect."[10]

Haiku is not the only medium through which Zen expresses itself in Japanese culture. "Today Buddhism has perished in India and is very inactive in China, but in Japan," states Zen master Kinei Otokawa, chief abbot of the Soto sect, Zen "... is vibrantly alive and very much a part of the daily life of the people. And it provides guidance for all levels of society."[11] Zen has entered almost all aspects of Japanese life and art—their poetry (haiku and tanka), calligraphy, architecture, painting (*Suni* and *Chinzo* portraiture), athletics (judo), landscape gardening (sand and rock gardens such as the one at Ryoanji in Kyoto), flower arrangement (*ikebana*) and, of course, the tea ceremony (*chanoyu*).

The spirit of Zen is within the tea ceremony to the Zen Buddhist, for it has the spirit of harmony, reverence, purity and tranquillity. Murato Shuko, the founder of the tea ceremony, taught that by raising the ordinary occurrences of life to an art the mind would be stilled and one would attain Buddha consciousness.

Zen is now a traditional religion in Japan with all the weaknesses of a religious institution. Zen is far less popular than other Japanese schools of Buddhism. Nevertheless Zen is the cornerstone of the Japanese culture and has touched every Japanese in some way.

The Japanese inherited Zen from the Chinese where it was known as Ch'an. The Chinese say that Ch'an is derived from the ancient Pali word *jhana*. Many state that Gautama himself gave birth to Zen. One day, they say, a Brahman approached the Buddha and offered him a golden flower. After he was asked to preach the Dharma (Law), the Buddha sat in silence and stared at the flower. Only Mahakasyapa understood his silence. The disciple responded with a smile, and thus the most precious Wisdom was transmitted from the Buddha to Mahakasyapa.

The twenty-eighth patriarch of Zen was the Indian philosopher Bodhidharma (480-528) who brought the principles and the techniques of Dhyana meditation to China in 520 during the Liang dynasty. After the death of Hung-Jen (605-75), the fifth successor to Bodhidharma, Zen (Ch'an) split into two schools—the northern sect which died out within a century and the southern sect which reached Japan within that same period.

Zen proliferated and split into many sects in Japan, but two that are noteworthy are Rinzai and Soto. In 1191, a Tendai monk named Eisai founded the Rinzai sect. Shortly afterward, another monk, Dogen, established the Soto sect. Most of the Zen masters who have immigrated to the United States have come from these two sects.

In 1893, Soyen Shaku was invited to the World's Parliament of Religions, which was held in Chicago. Soyen Shaku was the first Zen master to promote the growth of Zen in this country. The success of Zen, however, was not due to him but rather to his disciple, Dr. Daisetz Teitaro Suzuki (1870-1966).

The writings of D. T. Suzuki are chiefly responsible for the popularity of Zen in the West. "Until the 1960s," says Emma Layman, "most of what the English-speaking world knew of Zen came from Suzuki's pen."[12] From 1950 to 1958, he lectured on Buddhism at Columbia University. These lectures, along with his many books on Zen, stimulated a lifelong interest in Zen Buddhism among such Westerners as Alan Watts and Christmas Humphreys. Although Suzuki was neither a Zen priest or master, as an adherent of the Rinzai sect, he taught that a quick, abrupt experience effects enlightenment contrary to the gradual process toward enlightenment which is the teaching of the Soto sect which has been more popular in Japan.

Other Easterners who have taught Zen in the West are

Sogaku Harada, Shinryu Suzuki and Dr. Kyung Beo Seo. Harada came from the Hosshin Temple in Japan and taught both the Rinzai and Soto techniques of Zen. The Eihei Temple in Japan commissioned Shinryu Suzuki to instruct Westerners on Soto Zen. Dr. Seo brought a Korean form of Zen Buddhism to America. Although the shadow of D. T. Suzuki has obscured the accomplishments of these men, they still have played significant roles in the development of Zen in the West.

There are also Westerners who have done much to advance Zen—most notably Alan Wilson Watts. Watts was born on January 15, 1915, in Chislehurst, England. At the age of twenty-three he came to the United States where he was ordained in 1944 as an Anglican priest. During the next decade, D. T. Suzuki had a substantial influence on Watts, whose faith moved from Christianity to Zen Buddhism. Watts has written a number of widely read books extolling the virtues of his understanding of Zen.

Philip Kapleau is another important figure. He, unlike most Westerners, has tried to adjust the traditional techniques of Zen into a more Western form. For example, he introduced English words into the practice of chanting. Since he is one of few Americans who has been ordained a Zen priest in Japan, his unique style of Zen has been generally observed with respect.

Zen has also influenced prominent Roman Catholics such as Dom Aelred Graham, a Benedictine scholar. He became deeply interested in Zen and wrote the book *Zen Catholicism.* Nevertheless, Zen has only recently enjoyed such favor. After the First Zen Institute of New York was established in 1930, only a few people joined the Institute during the next two decades. Most people who had any interest in Buddhism prior to the late forties were Asian-Americans. Not until the middle fifties did Zen begin to have a wide following.

Outside the mainstream of American Zen during the late fifties, groups of philosophers, artists, poets and students extracted the existential tendencies of Zen. This brand of Zen was known as "Beat Zen," and its spokesman was the Beat novelist Jack Kerouac.

Although only a half-dozen Zen monasteries have been established in the United States, and although many people have deserted Zen, a growing number of Zen masters are forming Zendos (Zen centers) and their own Zen meditation groups. Zen may not seem to the media to be as fascinating as it was during the late fifties and early sixties, but actually Zen is now penetrating American philosophy and art much more deeply.

Zen itself cannot be defined because it has no definition. Its philosophy cannot be delineated because it has no theory or system of principles. "Zen is beyond description,"[13] says Christmas Humphreys. "Zen is not something that can be explained in words," says Toichi Yoshioka, "but is a practice which is carried out for one's own self-development and leads to a state of liberation called satori."[14] Alan Watts states that the Tao is beyond words in reference to the Zen experience: "To say that 'everything is the Tao'[15] almost gets the point, but just at the moment of getting it, the words crumble into nonsense. For we are here at a limit at which words break down because they always imply a meaning beyond themselves—and here there is no meaning beyond."[16]

If Zen cannot be defined or described, then at least the effort has been attempted countless times. Within the past two decades a mountain of literature has appeared in American bookstores. Most of these books deal with, sometimes in caricature, the highest concern of Zen—not the mode of Zen's expression but its experience. "It is enough to add," says Alan Watts, "that Zen is first and last a matter of experience."[17] "Personal experience," says D. T. Suzuki, "is everything in Zen."[18] For him, the experience of Zen cuts through rational authority and objective revelation and unveils spiritual truth. He then argues that Zazen is "the most practical method of attaining spiritual enlightenment."[19]

Za means sitting and *Zen* means meditation. Zazen, like Zen, cannot be explained. Dogen states in *Fukan Zazengi (The Universal Promotion of the Principles of Zazen)* that the crux of Zazen is "non-thinking; that is the essential art of Zazen." Since non-thinking is non-thinking, to explain non-thinking would automatically mean that it is not non-thinking. Therefore Zazen must be something which can only be experienced for yourself.

Zen Buddhism seeks Truth through meditation, and Zazen can only be performed through self-effort (*jiriki*). "You yourself must make the effort," says the *Dhammapada*. "Buddhas do but point the way." In other words, the Zen Buddhist must have faith in his own Buddha-nature. To have faith in the Buddha is irrelevant. In fact there are Zen stories of the images and icons of the Buddha being burned or desecrated. Even the name of the Buddha has been referred to as dung. The Roshi (Zen master) employs these apparent profanities in order to teach the disciple that "one does not practice Zen to become a Buddha; one practices it because one is a Buddha from the beginning."[20] The Zen Buddhist must not look to the Buddha but know that he is a Buddha himself. "For Buddha's sake Buddha is to be given up. This is the only way to come to the realization of the truth of Zen."[21]

The ultimate goal of the Zen Buddhist is the same as for

all Buddhists: the attainment of nirvana, which is the extinction of all desires and passions and the extinction of the individual identity. The immediate goal of the Zen Buddhist, however, is uniquely Zen: *satori*, which is an experiential realization that duality is the illusion of the mind that comes when all is perceived as one. *Satori* is an inner perception of reality. It is "the heart of Zen."

Two techniques are employed in the Rinzai sect of Zen Buddhism to attain *satori*. The rapid exchange between master and disciple through question and answer is a technique known as *mondo*. The other technique is the concentration on a *koan*, a phrase or problem which is insoluble to the intellect. Both are in frequent use in the West:

"Is there Buddha-nature in a dog?" "When your mind is not dwelling on good and evil, what is your original face before you were born?" "The sound of one hand clapping." "All things are such as they are from the beginning; what is that which is beyond existence?"

These famous *koans* are four of an estimated 1,700. Only a few, however, are necessary to reach *satori*. Only one may be enough. When one solves his *koan*, and not by reason, he experiences *kensho* (Enlightenment). Each *kensho* will transport the individual to a higher state of *satori*.

Although the *koan* is a Zen paradox whose expression goes beyond conceptual reasoning, "the Koan is neither a riddle nor a witty remark," states D. T. Suzuki. "It has a most definite objective, the arousing of doubt and pushing it to its furthest limits."[22] *Koans*, therefore, are used as a means to cut through discriminating intellect in order to achieve *satori*.

For different people, Zen Buddhism means different things. For some, Zen "creates compassion, and it creates detachment."[23] For others, Zen "is at once, the Life, the

Truth, and the Way."[24] And for still others, Zen is the frog jumping into an old pond. Plop!

SIX

Jesus Christ

BUDDHISM AND CHRISTIANITY: two religions to which I have always been exposed. It is not surprising, therefore, that I had to make a choice between them early in my life. And yet, I cannot help but look back now and then to see where I might have gone if I had chosen differently. What may be surprising is that today I am a Christian. Naturally, if I would have become a Buddhist, I would be in a situation very different from where I am now. But that I have become a Christian I attribute to Jesus Christ and to him alone.

A Question of Suffering
In the fifties, I grew up in a nearly all-white neighborhood

in California. Because I was of Japanese descent, and because the last World War was still vivid in most people's minds, I received regular physical and verbal abuse. I still remember the times when I was on the ground being kicked, or in a center of a ring of rock-throwers, or when my new clothes were muddied. But worse than the physical abuse were the verbal accusations. I felt even more defenseless against the charges that my family had attacked Pearl Harbor.

It is not easy for me to confess that I suffered deeply, but I did. Frequently I would try to wash my skin over and over again so that it might be as white as my schoolmates, but I could not escape racial prejudice in this way. Instead, I kept as far away from people as I could, and experienced another type of suffering which cut even deeper. When it is constant, loneliness can be the worst and best companion in a person's childhood. Loneliness for me was my most dreaded friend.

How to deal with my suffering from prejudice, loneliness, and yes, self-pity, became my daily preoccupation as I grew up. I had to face it lest I became emotionally scarred for the rest of my life. Two ways were open to me. They presented themselves not in answers but in images: the image of the serene Buddha and the image of Christ on the cross.

I must be honest and say that I had no real understanding of who the Buddha was or what his teachings were. Rather, my image of the Buddha came to me in the real form of my father's father, who possessed all the admirable qualities which Buddhism teaches. My grandfather was a devout Buddhist who taught his children to be good Buddhists. He was also a man who had suffered, and, moreover, suffered from prejudice. But he overcame, and he overcame through Buddhism. He was serene and peaceful, a true reflection of the Buddha.

It is not surprising to me that many people such as my grandfather have chosen to emulate the Buddha. "The figure of the founder of Buddhism," states Stephen Neill, a bishop in the Anglican Church, "a little romanticized, but, as we have seen, not very far from the historical reality, is full of charm. It presents precisely that quality which modern man knows himself to lack—serenity."[1] Bishop Neill goes on to point out that people are not only involved in an "ardent quest in search of reality, of an inner understanding of the truth of all things"[2] but also in an escape from their sufferings. Thus, "if desire can but be eliminated, release from suffering will be possible and then men's quest will be at an end."[3]

In the Second Holy Truth, the Buddha taught that human desire leads to suffering and that the desire to affirm the lower self is evil. He then taught how human desires can be eliminated and how release from suffering can be possible. My grandfather devoted his entire life to the teachings of the Buddha. He suppressed evil thoughts and desires, and the fruit of his efforts was that he became serene and gentle. I could have dealt with my suffering as my grandfather dealt with his, but there was still another way.

Very early in my life, my mother taught me to pray daily on my knees to God through his Son, Jesus Christ. I would use those times to release all the anguish of my soul to God, and I would channel all my sufferings through Christ. As I did, I became more and more aware of the image of Christ on the cross.

As I grew in my knowledge of Christ, I learned that people had also rejected him. They had abused him physically and verbally. They beat him and whipped him, and they bloodied his clothes. They had even accused him of being demon possessed. When he suffered terrible physical pain on the cross, they mocked him with words which I believe were even more painful for him to bear. On the cross he was utterly alone, for his disciples had abandoned him. But Christ was God. Just as he purposely became a man, he could have used his power as God to escape the cross, but he did not. Rather, he suffered, and I knew that he had suffered for me.

When he saw the tomb in which Lazarus, his friend, was buried, and when he saw the people crying because of Lazarus's death, Jesus wept. He did not hold back the tears; he did not suppress his emotions; he allowed his love to feel the anguish of others as well as his own anguish. But, again, Christ had the power of God. He could have delivered Lazarus from his sickness and not allowed Lazarus to die. But, although Christ accepts suffering, he does not succumb to it. Although he willingly suffers, he does not allow it to rule over his own will and deter him from doing God's will. Christ had allowed death to overcome Lazarus so that God might be glorified when he raised Lazarus from the tomb. Christ wept, but he also performed a miracle; and from what Christ did, there was great rejoicing.

The way which Christ dealt with suffering was another way which I could have dealt with mine. And so, I had two ways before me in which to go beyond my suffering: the way of the Buddha and the way of Christ. Bishop Neill portrays this contrast well:

Why suffer? That is the ultimate question. It comes to sharp and challenging expression in the contrast between the serene and passionless Buddha and the tortured figure on the Cross. In Jesus we see One who looked at suffering with eyes as clear and calm as those of the Buddha. He saw no reason to reject it, to refuse it, to eliminate it. He took it into himself and felt the fullness of its bitterness and horror; by the grace of God he tasted death for every man. Others suffer; he will suffer with them and for them, and will go on suffering till the end of time. But he does not believe that suffering is wholly evil; by the power of God it can be transformed into a redemptive miracle. Suffering is not an obstacle to deliverance, it can become part of deliverance itself. And what he was he bids his children be—the world's sufferers, in order that through suffering the world may be brought back to God.

The Buddhist ideal is that of passionless benevolence. The Christian ideal is that of compassion. When argument has done its best, we must perhaps leave the two ideals face to face. We can only ask our Buddhist friend to look long and earnestly on the Cross of Christ, and to ask himself whether, beyond the peace of the Buddha, there may not be another dimension of peace to the attainment of which there is no way other than the Way of the Cross.[4]

When I need to share something which causes me deep personal hurt, I go to people who I know have suffered from a similar experience and have gained wisdom from that experience. That is why I have always gone to Christ. I see in him someone who not only knows exactly what I am experiencing but feels what I feel, as well. I also see in him not one whom suffering has overcome but who has overcome suffering. Sometimes the joy is immediate; sometimes the joy takes years. In Christ's timetable, the joy does come, just as it did when Christ brought Lazarus back to life. But, whether or not the joy comes immediately, I have always found Christ's hand reaching for me whenever I am suffering, and for me this has been my only solace.

Different Paths to Different Summits

Masaharu Anesaki, professor of Japanese studies at Harvard University, writes: "There are many paths and roads in forests and valleys, but those who have climbed up to the hilltop by any of these routes equally enjoy the same moonlight on the open summit."[5] Anesaki has quoted an old Buddhist proverb. He has also articulated what many people believe: all religions essentially are the same. Different religions may guide people along different paths but they all lead ultimately to the same goal or, in this case, summit.

If Buddhism and Christianity are essentially the same, why did I become a Christian, especially when my family background was Buddhist and my grandfather was a devout Buddhist whom I highly respected? Did I become a Christian simply because the Christian path appealed more to me, knowing that the Christian path would bring me ultimately to the same end as the Buddhist path? The answer is that I saw not only that the paths veered in different directions but that the goals of each path were different as well.

It should be clear by now that Buddhism is not monolithic. If I had taken the Amidist path, it would have been different from the path of Zen. Buddhism is not a single, uniform philosophy with tenets consistent throughout all its schools and sects; neither is it a religion which stresses one form of worship or one system of belief; nor is it a discipline with one set of ethics. Even within Confucianism there are some who believe in the depravity of humanity and others in the inherent goodness of humanity. Theravada Buddhists are generally atheists, yet many Mahayana Buddhists have evolved a pantheon of gods (Buddhas and Bodhisattvas). In Amidism, only the grace and compassion of the Buddha can save the believer; in Zen Buddhism, self-effort delivers one from karma. Even within Buddhism there are many paths.

Nevertheless, different Buddhists, representing various Buddhist schools, do reach the same summit. They may differ on their selective paths but their chosen goal is the same, for there are basic characteristics which are consistent through each of the Buddhist schools that bind them all together in their spiritual quest. These characteristics are the Buddhist understanding of samsara (the continuous round of death and rebirth), karma (the law of cause and effect) and nirvana (extinction).

Christianity, meanwhile, is also not monolithic in structure, worship and doctrine. There are many Christian denominations and independent churches. There is elaborate liturgy in the Episcopal Church; there is a marked simplicity in the worship of the Baptists. There are various Christian doctrines on baptism and communion. And yet, Christianity also has basic characteristics which are not only consistent throughout orthodox Christianity but are in contrast to the Buddhist presuppositions concerning samsara, karma and nirvana.

Samsara's doctrine of death and rebirth gives an interesting answer to the haunting question: "Is there life beyond the grave?" To believe that one has lived before and will live again relieves the despair of life's present sufferings. It therefore follows that the human spirit would seek in samsara an answer to life's seeming temporality.

However hopeful a person might be for a better life in the future, the fact that life will be no different from the current life can only drag a person into deeper despair; life is nothing more than the sum total of all the physical and emotional problems which everyone must experience. Friedrich

Nietzsche vividly portrays this haunting theme on life after life:

> How, if some day or night a demon were to sneak after you into your loneliest loneliness and say to you, "This life as you now live it and have lived it, you will have to live once more and innumerable times more; and there will be nothing new in it. . . ." The question in each and every thing, "Do you want this once more and innumerable times more?" would weigh upon your actions as the greatest stress.[6]

This was the conclusion to which the Buddha came regarding samsara. And so, samsara becomes a curse rather than a solace for humanity; it chains people to eternal sufferings rather than frees them from the bondage of pain.

The Buddha did not continue in despair. He offered a way by which to break the chain of samsara, to sever people from their despair. If desires are the links of that chain, then each desire must be eliminated. The Buddha spoke of the way in the Noble Eightfold Path. To follow this path is to be delivered from suffering, from samsara, from the cycle of death and rebirth, from life itself.

Christianity also hopes for another life. "In our sad condition," said Martin Luther, "our only consolation is the expectancy of another life."[7] Christianity, however, does not hold to samsara. My life is not to be born again from a woman's womb but to live eternally according to the judgment of God. And it is in Christ I have my hope. Eternal life beyond the grave can be either heaven or hell, but in Christ heaven is promised.

"And just as it is appointed for men to die once, and after that comes judgment, so Christ, having been offered once to bear the sins of many, will appear a second time . . ." (Heb

9:27-28). What is significant about these verses from the Bible is not merely that I have one life and one death but that Jesus has died for me. This places the question of life and death in the most personal of terms. I am not faced with the impersonal process of death and rebirth armed only with the hope of "extinction." Rather, I am faced with a personal God whose concern and love for me are so great that he does not abandon me in my despair, nor did he spare his own Son. Instead he gave Christ up for me. "For God so loved the world that he gave his only Son, that whoever believes in him should not perish but have eternal life" (Jn 3:16).

The second Buddhist presupposition is its understanding of karma. Quite frankly, I find it a very attractive doctrine. Who does not yearn for justice in a world full of sorrow? *Fiat justitia, ruat coelum*—"justice be done, though the heavens fall in ruin." To right the wrongs both within and outside one's self is one of our deep yearnings. When we realize that we are impotent to do so, we cling to the hope of a greater power which *can*. For many, belief in karma answers that need.

All is subject to the universal law of karma. The actions of the past determine today; the actions of yesterday and today determine the future. Dr. Luan Suriyabongs says:

The law of karma is immensely reasonable and just. If man is solely responsible for his doings, and the effects of his doings cannot be expected to exhaust themselves in the span of a single life it is only just and fair that he should be given a chance to make good for the evil he has done, that is, that he should be reborn. By the same reasoning, it is also just and fair that the one to whom he owes a moral debt should likewise return to earth so that both can meet and their reciprocal karma exhaust itself.[8]

If karma is an impersonal force, however, then people themselves find it quite easy to become impersonal concerning their own actions. And so, they say: "It was my karma which made me do it." Or, "I am who I am because of my karma." Karma focuses on the responsibility of individuals for their own actions but, because it is an impersonal force, it allows people to disregard both the responsibility and the consequence of their own actions.

A devout Buddhist, however, earnestly seeks to escape his or her karma either by self-effort or through the compassion of Amida Buddha. Karma becomes not justice but a dispenser of pain and sorrow. Although karma is impersonal, it is a reality. One escapes karma only by escaping life. The ultimate resolution of karma is the cessation of life, and this is accomplished when the scales of karma are in balance. Buddhist justice, therefore, is not only deliverance from the sufferings of life but deliverance from life itself.

As a Christian I too yearn for justice, not only that I may be just but that there might be justice in the world. Whenever God called people to repent of their sins, he always called for justice to be practiced among people. He not only wanted people to live righteously but he also demanded that the poor be relieved, the oppressed be delivered and the orphaned be cared for. God sought through his people to "let justice roll down like waters, and righteousness like an ever-flowing stream" (Amos 5:24).

I think that both Buddhists and Christians understand and yearn for the type of justice which God calls for in people and in the world. But where Buddhists and Christians depart is in their response to Jesus Christ. For Buddhists, Christ is not necessary in their deliverance from karma, in their attainment of nirvana, and therefore in the resolution of justice as they see it. For Christians, there can be no righteousness, no justice without Christ. I do not have in myself strength enough, determination enough, power enough to live righteously or to become just. But Christ has come that both might happen.

"The Spirit of the Lord is upon me," said Christ, "because he has anointed me to preach good news to the poor. He has sent me to proclaim release to the captives and recovering of sight to the blind, to set at liberty those who are oppressed, to proclaim the acceptable year of the Lord" (Lk 4:18-19). Christ is not an impersonal force like karma which returns good for good and evil for evil; he is the ruler over all life who has personally lived and died among people. And because he lived righteously and triumphed over death by bodily returning from the grave, he has secured justice in heaven for those who love him.

Furthermore, justice is not only reserved in heaven but is also demanded for life on earth. "Thy will be done on earth as it is in heaven," Christ prayed to God his Father. As a Christian, I am accountable to be just; but also as a Christian, Christ has given me the power to be just. Not only will there be justice at the summit but Christ shall mark my path with righteousness and justice.

And so, our paths continue to diverge. For the Buddhists, the precepts of the Buddha help them in their search for a path which puts an end to samsara and a resolution of karma. For me as a Christian, Christ has found me and guides me along another path, one which seeks no escape from life. We are led, therefore, to different summits. For the Buddhists, the summit is nirvana; for me, the summit is heaven.

The Buddhist definition of nirvana captures the essence of death's beauty, if there is any beauty in death. There is no beginning; there is no end. There is no Creator; there is no Savior. The universe is in a flux. It is a fleeting process of arising and ceasing in an endless chain of causes and effects which are all interdependent. And karma binds all life to the cycle of rebirth so that life goes on and on in anguish. Nirvana, however, delivers a death which is not part of the cycle of death and rebirth but the ultimate death which is the extinction of life. Nirvana extinguishes the light of life which flickers in the darkness of sorrow. Nirvana is the highest goal of the Buddhist.

The Christian, however, views death very differently. Death is a curse which people must suffer because they have rejected the living God. The power of evil is death and the ultimate consequence of sin is the grave. The Christian, therefore, regards death as an enemy along with evil and sin. "For he [Christ] must reign until he has put all his enemies under his feet," says the Bible. "The last enemy to be destroyed is death" (1 Cor 15:25-26). Not only is death counted as an enemy of Christ but also Christ shall destroy death itself. Through his resurrection, Christ defeated the forces of evil. Christ was crucified on the cross, but he overcame death and was raised from the tomb. Death has been swallowed up in Christ's victory and, thus, death is no longer a curse for me.

I seek a path which leads away from despair, away from injustice, away from evil and sin, but I also seek a path which leads to life. Jesus Christ has found me. He does not guide me along a path which is without suffering, but he has prepared a place for me, a place beyond the sorrows of life, a place of eternal life in heaven with him. "Behold, the dwelling of God is with men. He will dwell with them, and they shall be his people, and God himself will be with them; he will wipe away every tear from their eyes, and death shall be no more, neither shall there be mourning nor crying nor pain any more, for the former things have passed away" (Rev 21:3-4).

In my quest for God, what path should I have taken? Should I have sought a path away from suffering to the summit of serenity? If I had, I would have taken a path different from the path which Christ has paved; his path is the way of the Cross, and all who travel it must suffer with him. If I had, I would discover a summit without Christ; Christ did not deny life, he affirmed it. Suffering for the sake of suffering? Of course not. Suffering because of my karma? I believe not. Rather, I share in Christ's suffering that people might live. I suffer that Christ might be glorified. It is in the fellowship of this suffering with Christ that my quest for God shall be fulfilled; for then I shall meet God on the summit and live with him forever.

Beyond the Grave

Although Buddhism and Christianity offer different paths and different summits, they cannot both be true. For if Buddhists hope for nothing beyond the grave, and if Christians are promised eternal life with God beyond the grave, then either one or the other or neither is true. The teachings of the Buddha and Jesus Christ cannot both be true.

Since my quest has always been to know God as my personal Creator, I cannot accept Buddhism. Buddhism offers many wonderful things, but it does not offer eternal life with a personal God who has made me as I am, physically and spiritually. "There is a need for fulfillment that is part of the stuff of life itself," writes Paul Tournier, "a need for personal adventure which is peculiar to man, a thirst for the absolute, which in the last analysis is an expression of man's hunger and thirst after God."[9] My hunger and my thirst cannot be satisfied in Buddhism because I know that the Buddha neither created me nor offers for me to live forever with him.

Several centuries ago, Augustine of North Africa also had this hunger and thirst to know God. "Thou hast formed us for Thyself," he said, "and our hearts are restless till they find rest in Thee."[10] Augustine finally found rest in Jesus Christ. In Christ, he found his Creator, his Savior and Lord. In Christ, I have also found my Creator, my Savior and Lord. The Bible tells me that in Christ "all things were created, in heaven and on earth, visible and invisible, whether thrones or dominions or principalities or authorities—all things were created through him and for him" (Col 1:16). The Bible also says: "For God has not destined us for wrath, but to obtain salvation through our Lord Jesus Christ, who died for us so that whether we wake or sleep we might live with him" (1 Thess 5:9-10). In this way I believe and have come to know my personal God, Jesus Christ.

The Bible speaks of a God beyond human wisdom. It speaks of a God who created me, who cared for me, who delivered me; a God beyond the furthest reaches of human thought and experience. But he remains a God who embraces those who seek him and gives them his thoughts and his experiences. The Bible speaks of a God beyond—who answers all questions, who satisfies all yearnings, who fulfills all needs. The God beyond is here in the person of Jesus.

I have given myself to Jesus Christ, and I have the assurance that beyond the grave my suffering shall be at an end and that I shall live with him forever. I know my God and am satisfied, but until the grave I still live in a world of suffering. Like a moon which is not full until it fully faces the sun, I shall not be full until I fully face the Son of God, Jesus Christ.

SEVEN

Reflections in Japan

ON THE BUDDHA'S BIRTHDAY, I was drinking *sakura-yu* in the evening in Kyoto. A storm had suddenly appeared during the day and had caused terrible havoc throughout central Japan. A train cable had been downed, and my passage from Nagoya to Kyoto was delayed several hours. After changing trains three times and arriving in Kyoto soaked to the skin, I finally had found sanctuary in a hot bath.

Now I sat in the hotel restaurant and reflected not only on the day's adventure but also on the various Shinto shrines and Buddhist temples I had seen the past week. The coming week, I knew, would take me to many more shrines and temples in the religious capital of Japan, Kyoto.

One of the shrines I had visited and had been captivated with was the Toshogu Shrine in Nikko. It had been dedicated to Tokugawa Ieyasu,[1] the founder of the Tokugawa shogunate and the great military hero of the late sixteenth and early seventeenth century. Standing near Tokugawa Ieyasu's mausoleum, awe-inspiring in its setting in the Nikko mountains, I had felt currents of conflicting feelings. Here was a great historical character from Japan's past, but here also was a man who did not believe in Christ and who lay still buried in his grave. Here was a magnificent monument dedicated to a national hero, worshiped as a god. But no monument or adoration can resurrect a man.

I have a deep love for the beauty of Japan. The cherry blossoms in Kyoto are the loveliest in the world, but they, like people, soon wither and die. Very few men have flowered to such a glory as Tokugawa Ieyasu, but even he had to die.

Allowing my thoughts to return to my tea and my present circumstances, I took the damp cherry blossom from my empty cup and placed it on the saucer.

The day's storm had prematurely swept the early blossoms away. As the week between the Buddha's birthday and Easter passed, more blossoms gathered on the trees in Kyoto. The days became warmer, and by the time Easter arrived the cherry trees were again in full bloom.

On Easter morning I visited a small Christian church with some friends. On the way we picked up a young Christian woman at the hospital. She smiled and laughed throughout our ride, and during that time I was told the testimony of her life.

She had come to know about Jesus through a missionary who was teaching her English. Later she accepted Jesus as her Lord and experienced severe hardship as a Christian.

Initially her family strongly protested her conversion, even forcing her to sit before a *Butsu-dan* and not allowing her to move until she renounced her faith. She finally succumbed to weariness and the oral pressures of her family. The next day she phoned a Christian friend and shared her deep guilt for having denied Christ. Her friend reminded her that Peter had denied Christ three times. The Lord blessed her with these words, for she not only was comforted, but like Peter, she also heard the Lord's call to feed his flock.

Several years of Christian service have passed and now she is slowly succumbing to a fatal disease. Her visits to the hospital are becoming more frequent and the pain is becoming more severe. And yet, she manifests the joy of Christ through it all. Many people have come to accept Christ by seeing his power and the victory in her life. Although her family still have not become Christians, they have received her back. Although her health is failing and she has experienced more suffering than any other member of her family, her mother declares that she is the happiest of them all.

After hearing this testimony, I was then told the story of a family who had been zealous Buddhists. One day, however, the eldest son became a believer in Christ. This disturbed the family, particularly the father. Many heated arguments ensued, but eventually one by one his brothers and sisters all became Christians. Later his father read the Bible in secret and came to realize that Buddhism has no cross, no salvation and no resurrection of the body. He had argued that Buddhism provides a high moral standard but now he saw that there was much more beyond Buddhism. And so, he too came to Christ.

The Buddhist priest and the village were appalled by his conversion. Here was a doctor, sixty years of age, who had been steeped in Buddhism. The conversion of a man in his position staggered the community. The priest warned him that disaster would fall on him and his family unless he recanted. Within months he contracted cancer, but he remained faithful to Christ. Later he was healed.

Nevertheless, tragedy soon struck the family again. His daughter, who was soon to be married, was killed in a car accident. The driver of the other car was at fault. The community had expected the disaster; they also expected his return to Buddhism. The tragedy occurred, but he still was faithful. As a matter of fact, he arranged the funeral service to be a time of celebration for he believed that she was now with the Lord. The mother became a Christian from this experience because she felt that heaven was so near. What amazed the community the most was that the family felt no hatred or bitterness toward the driver of the other car. They did not seek revenge but prayed for his salvation. This attitude was so contrary to what was expected that it seemed that a greater power was the cause of such a love.

While visiting the gorgeous shrines and elaborate temples of Japan, I could not help but feel that something was lacking in these holy places of worship. The historical Buddha certainly taught a high ethical morality. The Amida Buddha certainly is a symbol of compassion and mercy. I could marvel at the beauty of the shrines and the temples. I could respect the reverence of its caretakers. I could even be inspired by the endeavor of this human project to elevate humanity to the state of divine purity. But from dust they were built and to dust they shall return, and all the thoughts which I have thought while studying Buddhism and all the feelings which I have felt while visiting the shrines and temples could never satisfy the yearning of my soul to know the one true

Creator. Beyond the Buddha is the void, and the void does not answer the needs of my humanity.

A few days after Easter, I stood on the crowded platform, waiting for the train to leave Kyoto for Tokyo. The cherry blossoms were all gone now, and I sensed that a glory had passed—the same feeling which I had at Tokugawa Ieyasu's mausoleum. Yet, I felt something deeper. I knew that someday Jesus would return and bring a glory greater than any person has seen, a glory which will never fade or pass, a glory of his love for us.

In Christ is life, a life of joy and peace throughout eternity, and his words, "Surely I will be with you always, to the very end of the age."

Notes

Chapter 2

[1]My primary source for the biography of Siddhartha Gautama is *The Life of Buddha as Legend and History* by Edward J. Thomas (London: Routledge and Kegan Paul, 1969).

[2]Devout Buddhists avoid the use of his personal name and refer to him as the Buddha.

[3]Theravadin tradition dates his birth at 623 B.C.

[4]Other accounts say that he was visited by eight Brahman holy men.

[5]Other texts give her such names as Yasohara, Bhaddakacca and Bimba.

[6]Other accounts say that he merely envisioned these four states of humanity.

[7]Other accounts say that he was born seven days before; others say that his mother conceived him that night.

[8]Some accounts say that his horse died of a broken heart and was reborn a god.

[9]The name "Mara" is found in Sanskrit accounts, outside of Buddhist texts, in the sense of "death" but not as a character.

[10]Christmas Humphreys, *Buddhism* (London: Penguin Books, 1951), p. 41.

[11]Edward J. Thomas, *The Life of Buddha as Legend and History* (London: Routledge and Kegan Paul, 1969), p. 193.

[12]Richard H. Robinson, *The Buddhist Religion*, The Religious Life of Man Series (Belmont, Calif.: Dickenson, 1970), p. 35.

[13]Edward Conze, *Buddhism: Its Essence and Development* (New York: Harper and Row, 1959), p. 58.

[14]Henri Arvon, *Buddhism* (New York: Walker and Co., 1962), p. 55.

[15]The Buddha's hostile attitude toward women has been dismissed as legendary by such scholars as M. E. Lulius van Goor. The accounts of the Buddha's treatment of women, however, at the very least must reflect an attitude which was held early in the Sangha.

Chapter 3

[1]Many scholars list Vajrayana as a varient of Mahayana.

[2]Arvon, p. 63.

[3]Scholars disagree on the date.

[4]There is an interesting debate as to whether the Theravadins are of the Hinayana, "the Small Vehicle." Naturally the Theravadins dismiss this term because of its derogatory implication. Lama Anagarika Govinda says that the Theravadins cannot be identified with the Hinayana since the Theravadins do not reject the Bodhisattva ideal; he also points out that the Hinayana died out early in Buddhist history (*Foundations of Tibetan Mysticism* [New York: E. P. Dutton & Co., 1960], p. 41). Beatrice L. Suzuki, however, although she agrees that the two are not necessarily the same, states that the Theravadins were the Primitive Buddhists who eventually divided into the Hinayana and the Mahayana. Most scholars, nevertheless, refer to Buddhism of the Southern countries as Theravada Buddhism, and so shall I (*Mahayana Buddhism* [New York: Macmillan Co., 1969]), p. 32.

[5]Suzuki, p. 21.

[6]Ibid., p. 15.

[7]Some scholars state that Sambhogakaya is like the Christian Christ. Other scholars state that the Buddha in this form has a close resemblance to God the Father in Christianity. Suzuki, however, sees a difference: "Amida's attitude towards sin is what distinguishes the Shinshu from Christianity. The God of the latter is a God of love and justice, while the Buddha is mercy itself and nothing more. In the world the

principle of karma prevails, and the Buddha never judges. The God of Judaism was represented by Christ to be the God of love, yet he is made to judge over our sins and mete out punishments accordingly" (ibid., p. 64).

[8]Ibid., pp. 52-63.

[9]In Japan, Buddhism is often divided into two ways of salvation: the Tariki sects (such as the Amidist schools) which stress salvation by faith; the Jiriki sects (such as the Shingon, Tendai and Zen schools) which stress Enlightenment through self-effort.

[10]Suzuki, p. 36.

[11]Govinda, p. 61.

[12]In Tibetan Buddhism, demons are numerous and ubiquitous, for they have an important role in Vajrayana Buddhism. Says John Blofeld, "... nightmarish figures in the sacred pictures, unlike gods and demons elsewhere, are recognized by the faithful as the products of their own minds" (*The Tantric Mysticism of Tibet* [New York: E. P. Dutton & Co., 1970], p. 88). They also help to purify the individual and accelerate his deliverance from ignorance. Needless to say, demons are not only welcomed but honored.

[13]For example: "Arya Tara personifies the saving power of Wisdom and Compassion. She has her right palm extended outwards and pointing down with thumb and fingers forming a circle to symbolize protecting power while her left hand is held palm outwards pointing upwards with thumb and middle fingers joined so that three fingers are erect, symbolizing the Three Precious Ones of which she is an emanation" (ibid., footnote on p. 88).

[14]Ibid., p. 74.

[15]The union of *upaya* and *prajna* is personified in Tibetan art, such as the illustration of the ecstatic embrace of the *Yabyun* (Father-Mother) figures, or the statues depicting the divine union between *Demchog* (highest bliss) and *Dorje Phasmo* (transcendental knowledge).

[16]Govinda, p. 90.

[17]Arvon, pp. 84-85.

[18]Lama Anagarika Govinda, *The Way of the White Clouds* (Berkeley: Shambhala, 1970), p. 23.

Chapter 4

[1]Robinson, pp. 41-42.

[2]Ibid., p. 77.

[3]Lionel Giles, *The Sayings of Confucius*, Wisdom of the East Series

(London: John Murray, 1917), p. 42.

[4]H. G. Creel (quoting Homer H. Dubs), *Chinese Thought from Confucius to Mao Tse-tung* (New York: Mentor, 1953), p. 98.

[5]Ibid., p. 233.

[6]Ibid., pp. 30-31.

[7]Ibid., p. 142.

[8]Ibid., p. 38.

[9]Ibid., p. 190.

[10]John B. Noss, *Man's Religions*, 2nd ed. (New York: Macmillan Co., 1956), p. 29.

[11]A totalitarian system of rule, politically and philosophically.

[12]Laura Pilarski, *Tibet: Heart of Asia* (Indianapolis: Bobbs-Merrill Co., 1974), p. 27.

[13]Tulku is a Tibetan term for a person who is recognized as the present incarnation of an exalted being.

[14]Pilarski, p. 44.

[15]Ibid., p. 90.

[16]Great Britain had finally given India her independence and now had no interest in Tibet. Because India did not want to offend the Chinese, she was following a policy of "abandonment of Tibet."

[17]Pilarski, p. 101.

[18]Ibid., p. 106.

[19]Some say that he wore monk's clothes.

[20]Pilarski, p. 112.

[21]Noss, p. 400 (footnote).

[22]Many Shinto believers also claim that the first emperor of Japan was a grandson of a god.

[23]Buddhism soon flourished under the patronage of Prince Shotoku (573-621), whom many consider to be the founder of Japanese Buddhism.

[24]Actually the Heian period, which followed the Nara period (710-794), is divided into three distinct periods: the Heian (794-866), the Fujiwara (866-1160) and the Taira (1160-1185).

[25]The established schools of Buddhism are commonly known as the Six Nara sects: the Jojitsu, the Sanron, the Hosso, the Kusha, the Ritsu and the Kegon.

[26]E. Dale Saunders, *Buddhism in Japan* (Philadelphia: University of Pennsylvania Press, 1971), p. 139.

[27]Although their depiction of the samurai were usually of the Tokugawa period (1600-1868), through Akira Kurosawa's direction and Toshiro Mifune's many roles as a samurai with faults and virtues struggling to

transcend his troubled world, the warrior has been tellingly represented on the cinematic screen. The courtier, with his cultivated manners and sophistication, has been portrayed vividly in *The Tale of Genji* by Lady Murasaki (978?-1031?).

[28]Saunders, p. 186.

[29]Zen Buddhism is discussed more extensively in chapter five.

[30]Saunders, p. 228.

[31]Ibid., p. 230.

[32]Also, the great Japanese poet Basho wrote his famous haiku during the seventeenth century. His haiku truly represent the Japanese consciousness and the essence of Zen.

Chapter 5

[1]Emma McCloy Layman, *Buddhism in America* (Chicago: Nelson-Hall, 1976), p. 49.

[2]Ibid., p. 133.

[3]*Time*, 17 September 1979, p. 96.

[4]Layman, p. 82.

[5]Ibid., p. 99.

[6]Govinda, *The Way of the White Clouds*, p. 72.

[7]Blofeld, p. 9.

[8]"Dalai Lama's on a pilgrimage to make friends," *Chicago Tribune*, 3 September 1979, reprinted with permission from *New York* magazine.

[9]R. H. Blyth, *Zen in English Literature and Oriental Classics* (Tokyo: Hokuseido Press, 1942), p. 217.

[10]D. T. Suzuki, *An Introduction to Zen Buddhism* (New York: Grove Press, 1964), p. 117.

[11]Toichi Yoshioka, *Zen* (Osaka, Japan: Hoikusha Pub. Co., 1978), p. 1.

[12]Layman, p. 28.

[13]Christmas Humphreys, *Zen Buddhism* (New York: Macmillan Co., 1970), p. 55.

[14]Yoshioka, p. 4.

[15]Many Zen Buddhists believe that some of the major tenets of Zen have sprung from Taoism.

[16]Alan Watts, *The Way of Zen* (New York: Pantheon Books, 1957), p. 147.

[17]Ibid., p. 26.

[18]D. T. Suzuki, p. 33.

[19]Ibid., p. 34.

[20]Watts, p. 154.

[21]D. T. Suzuki, pp. 54-55.

[22]Ibid., p. 108.

[23]Janwillem van de Wetering, *The Empty Mirror* (New York: Kangaroo Books, 1978), p. 176.

[24]Humphreys, *Zen Buddhism*, p. 11.

Chapter 6

[1]Stephen Neill, *Christian Faith and Other Religions* (London: Oxford University Press, 1970), p. 113.

[2]Ibid., p. 99.

[3]Ibid., p. 100.

[4]Ibid., pp. 123-24.

[5]Masaharu Anesaki, "How Christianity Appeals to a Japanese Buddhist," *Hibbert Journal*, vol. iv, no. 1, (1905).

[6]Friedrich Nietzsche, *The Portable Nietzsche*, ed. Walter Kaufman (New York: Penguin Books, 1976), p. 101.

[7]Martin Luther, *Table Talk of Martin Luther*, ed. Thomas S. Kepler (Grand Rapids: Baker, 1979), p. 132.

[8]Luan Suriyabongs, *Buddhism in the Light of Modern Scientific Ideas*, rev. ed. (Bangkok: Nai Pinich Oosamran, 1960), p. 73.

[9]Paul Tournier, *The Adventure of Living* (New York: Harper and Row, 1965), p. 9.

[10]Augustine, *Confessions*, trans. F. J. Sheed (New York: Sheed & Ward, 1943), p. 3.

Chapter 7

[1]Surnames are often listed first in Japanese.

Bibliography

General Buddhism

Arvon, Henri. *Buddhism*. New York: Walker and Company, 1962.

Comstock, W. Richard, ed. *Religion and Man*. New York: Harper and Row, 1951.

Conze, Edward. *Buddhism, Its Essence and Development*. New York: Harper and Row, 1951.

——————. *Buddhist Texts Through the Ages*. New York: Harper and Row, 1954.

Guenther, Herbert V. *Buddhist Philosophy in Theory and Practice*. Middlesex, England: Penguin Books, 1971.

Noss, John B. *Man's Religions*. New York: The Macmillan Company, five editions.

Robinson, Richard H. *The Buddhist Religion*. Belmont, Calif.: Dickenson Publishing, 1970.

Smart, Ninian. *The Religious Experience of Mankind*. New York: Charles

Scribner's Sons, 1969.

Tomlin, E. W. F. *The Eastern Philosophers*, chapter five. London: Hutchinson and Company, 1968.

Indian Buddhism

Baird, Robert D. and Alfred Bloom. *Indian and Far Eastern Religious Traditions*. New York: Harper and Row, 1972.

Basham, A. L. *The Wonder That Was Indian*. New York: Grove Press, 1954.

Burh, E. A., ed. *The Teachings of the Compassionate Buddha*. New York: Mentor, 1955.

Conze, Edward, ed. *Buddhist Scriptures*. London: Penguin Books, 1959.

_____ . *Buddhist Thought in India*. Ann Arbor: University of Michigan Press, 1967.

Dasgupta, Surendranath. *A History of Indian Philosophy*. 3 vols. London: Cambridge University Press, 1932.

Eliot, Sir Charles. *Hinduism and Buddhism*. London: Arnold, 1921.

Kitagawa, Joseph M. *Religions of the East*. Philadelphia: Westminster, 1960.

Morgan, Kenneth. *The Path of the Buddha*. New York: Ronald, 1956.

Mascaro, Juan, trans. *The Dhammapada*. Middlesex, England: Penguin Books, 1973.

Thomas, Edward J. *The Life of Buddha as Legend and History*. London: Routledge and Kegal Paul, 1927.

_____ . *The Road to Nirvana*. London: Butler and Tanner, 1950.

Chinese Buddhism

Ch'en, Kenneth. *Buddhism in China: A Historical Survey*. Princeton: Princeton University Press.

Chung-Yuan, Chang. *Original Teachings of Chan Buddhism*. New York: Vintage Books, 1975.

Creel, H. G. *Chinese Thought from Confucius to Mao Tse-Tung*. New York: Mentor, 1953.

De Bary, William Theodore. *Sources of Chinese Tradition*. New York: Columbia, 1960.

Fung, Yu-Lan. *History of Chinese Philosophy*. tr. by Derk Bodde. 2 volumes. Princeton: Princeton University Press, 1952-53.

Giles, Lionel. *The Sayings of Confucius*. London: John Murray, 1917.

Lao Tzu. trans. R. B. Blakney. *The Way of Life*. New York: Mentor Books, 1955.

Waley, Arthur, trans. *The Analects of Confucius*. New York: Vintage Books, 1938.

Wilhelm, Richard and Beynes, Cary F., trans. *The I Ching.* Princeton: Princeton University Press, 1950.

Wright, Arthur F. *Buddhism in Chinese History.* Stanford: Stanford University Press, 1959.

Yang, C. K. *Religion in Chinese Society.* Berkeley: University of California Press, 1970.

Tibetan Buddhism

Bell, Sir Charles. *The Religion of Tibet.* Oxford: Oxford University Press, 1931.

Blofeld, John. *The Tantric Mysticism of Tibet.* New York: E. P. Dutton & Co., 1970.

David-Neel, Alexandra and Lama Yongden. *The Secret Oral Teachings in Tibetan Buddhist Sects.* San Francisco: City Lights Books, 1967.

——————. *Magic and Mystery in Tibet.* Great Britain: Corgi, 1965.

Evans-Wentz, W.Y. *The Tibetan Book of the Dead.* London: Oxford University Press, 1964.

——————. *The Tibetan Book of the Great Liberation.* London: Oxford University Press, 1960.

——————. *Tibet's Great Yogi Milarepa.* London: Oxford University Press, 1928.

Govinda, Lama Anagarika. *Foundations of Tibetan Mysticism.* New York: E. P. Dutton & Co., 1960.

——————. *The Way of the White Clouds.* Berkeley: Shambhala, 1970.

Pilarski, Laura. *Tibet: Heart of Asia.* Indianapolis: Bobbs-Merrill, 1974.

Trungpa, Chogyam. *Born in Tibet.* London: George Allen and Unwin, 1966.

——————. *Cutting Through Spiritual Materialism.* Berkeley: Shambhala, 1973.

Waddell, L. A. *The Buddhism of Tibet or Lamaism.* Cambridge: Heffner, 1943.

Japanese Buddhism

Barret, William, ed. *Zen Buddhism: Selected Writings of D. T. Suzuki.* Garden City, N.Y.: Doubleday, 1956.

De Bary, William Theodore, ed. *Sources of Japanese Traditions.* New York: Columbia University Press, 1958.

Earhart, H. Byron. *Japanese Religion: Unity and Diversity.* Belmont, Calif.: Dickenson Publishing, 1969.

Eliot, Charles. *Japanese Buddhism.* New York: Barnes and Noble, 1967.

Kitagawa, Joseph M. *Religion in Japanese History.* New York: Columbia University, 1968.

Murata, Kiyoaki. *Japan's New Buddhism: An Objective Account of Soka Gakkai*. New York and Tokyo: John Weatherhill, 1969.

Saunders, E. Dale. *Buddhism in Japan*. Philadelphia: University of Pennsylvania Press, 1964.

Suzuki, Beatrice Lane. *Mahayana Buddhism*. Toronto, Canada: Macmillan Co., 1959.

Takakuso, Junjiro. *The Essentials of Buddhist Philosophy*. Honolulu: University of Hawaii Press, 1947.

Thomsen, Harry. *The New Religions of Japan*. Rutland, Vt.: Tuttle, 1963.

American Buddhism

Clark, David K. *The Pantheism of Alan Watts*. Downers Grove: InterVarsity Press, 1978.

Humphreys, Christmas. *Zen Buddhism*. London: Allen and Unwin, 1957.

Layman, Emma McCloy. *Buddhism in America*. Chicago: Nelson-Hall, 1976.

Needleman, Jacob. *The New Religions*. Garden City, N.Y.: Doubleday, 1970.

Roszak, Theodore. *The Making of a Counterculture*. Garden City, N.Y.: Doubleday, 1969 (esp. chapter one).

The Buddhist Churches of America. San Francisco: Buddhist Churches of America, 1971.

Watts, Alan W. *The Way of Zen*. New York: Pantheon Books, 1959.

Glossary

ABHIDHAMMA: the analysis of the philosophy and psychology of Buddhism.

AJARI: a spiritual master in the Shugendo sect of Japanese Buddhism, adept in ascetic practices.

AMIDISM: salvation by grace through faith in the Amida Buddha.

ARHAT: a person who has accomplished the Four Holy Truths in Theravada Buddhism.

ATMAN: the inner essence of a person.

BODHISATTVA: a being who seeks Enlightenment but delays Buddhahood in order to save others first with his own merits.

BUDDHA: a person who has experienced Enlightenment, or specifically Siddhartha Gautama, the founder of Buddhism.

BUTSU-DAN: a Buddha-shelf in homes of Buddhists. A place where the family worships and brings offerings such as fruit, flowers and rice.

CHRIST: the anointed one or the Messiah who was prophesied in the Old

Testament; specifically, Jesus of Nazareth, the founder of Christianity.
CHUN TZU: the Chinese ideal of a gentleman.
DAIKYO: "Great Doctrine."
DAIMOKU: an invocation.
DHARMA: a word with complex meanings, it normally refers to the teachings of the Buddha.
DHARMAKAYA: the Universal Buddha.
EIGHTFOLD PATH: the fourth of the Four Holy Truths.
ENLIGHTENMENT: the revelation of Truth.
GOHONZON: a small Buddhist altar.
HAIKU: a three-line, seventeen-syllable, Japanese poem.
HINAYANA: literally, "the little or lesser vehicle." To the Theravadists it is a disparaging term.
I CHING: "the book of changes," which deals with methods of divination.
JIRIKI: the way of salvation by "self-effort" in the Japanese schools of Buddhism, such as Zen Buddhism.
KAMI-NO-MICHI: "Way of the Gods."
KARMA: the law of cause and effect; a doctrine that a person's actions of the past govern the present life, and that past and present actions govern future lives.
KENSHO: in Zen Buddhism, "Enlightenment."
KOAN: a statement which cannot be resolved or understood by the intellect in order to cut through the rational process of the mind to achieve Enlightenment.
LAMA: a priest or monk in Lamaism or Tibetan Buddhism.
MAHAYANA: literally, "the great vehicle"; Buddhism of the Northern School.
MANDALA: in Buddhism, a mystical representation of the cosmic universe with the Buddha at the center and other figures surrounding him.
MANTRAS: the verbal formulas employed to effect spiritual power.
MONDO: in Zen Buddhism, the rapid exchange between master and disciple in order to effect Enlightenment of the disciple.
MUDRA: the bodily gestures which accompany meditation, particularly hand and finger positions.
NIRMANAKAYA: the historical Buddha.
NIRVANA: literally, the "void"; the attainment of Enlightenment during life; the annihilation of the separate self at death.
OBON: from the word *Urabon* ("being hung upside down"); the "Festival of Joy."

PATIVEDHANANA: the Four Holy Truths or the Four Noble Truths; the universality of suffering; the cause of suffering; the annihilation of suffering; the Eightfold Path to eradicate attachment.

PRAJNA: the female, passive principle, expressed in terms of "wisdom."

PRAYER-WHEEL or *MANI-CHO-KHOR:* an aid in meditation in concentrating upon a mantra, symbolizing the turning of the wheel of the Dharma.

RESURRECTION: the state of having risen from the dead; specifically, the rising of Jesus from the dead.

RIGHTEOUSNESS: being just and morally good.

RINPOCHE: a leader in Tibetan Buddhism.

ROSHI: a Zen master.

SAKURU-YU: cherry blossom tea.

SAMBHOGAKAYA: the eternal Buddha or the Buddha ideal.

SAMSARA: literally, "wheel-turning"; the continuous round of death and rebirth.

SANGHA: specifically, the Buddhist monastic order; generally, the society of Buddhist believers.

SATORI: state of Enlightenment in Zen Buddhism.

SHAKTISM: the religion in which duality is divided into male and female elements such as power, deities and sexuality.

SHAMANISM: a belief in good and evil spirits who can be influenced by a priest or medicine man.

SHINTO: "Way of the Gods."

SHOGUN: the military leader who controls the political and social life of Japan.

SUNYATA or *SUNYA:* the Void or emptiness.

SUTRAS or *SUTTRAS:* sermons or discourses.

TANTRISM: the mystical nature of esoteric Buddhism, utilizing such techniques as mantras, yantras and mudras.

TAO: a concept with complex meanings not definable in words for the Chinese, but generally, "the Way."

TAO TE CHING: the book of the Virtuous Way.

TARIKI: the way of salvation, not by self-effort, but by the power of an external force in the Japanese schools of Buddhism such as the Amidist schools.

THERAVADA: "the Doctrine of the Elders"; the fundamentalist branch of Buddhism; the Southern school of Buddhism.

TRIKAYA: the three manifestations of the Buddha: Nirmanakaya, Sambhogakaya and Dharmakaya.

TRIPITAKA: the three baskets composed of the Vinaya-pitaka (the rules of discipline of the Order), the Sutta-pitaka (sermons of the Buddha) and the Abhidhamma (philosophical commentaries on the teachings of the Buddha); the three main divisions of the Pali Canon.

UPAYA: the male, active principle, expressed in terms of "love and compassion."

VAJRAYANA: literally, "the Diamond Vehicle"; the Tantric form of Buddhism, prevalent in Tibet as Lamaism; a derivation of Mahayana Buddhism.

VINAYA: rules and regulations within the Buddhist order.

YAMABUSHI: "ones who lie down or sleep in the mountains."

YANA: "vehicle," or the path one progresses to nirvana.

YANG: the male, active principle in Taoism.

YANTRAS: visual techniques of meditation of which the mandala is of special use.

YIN: the female, passive principle in Taoism.

ZAZEN: meditation in a seated position in Zen Buddhism.

ZENDOS: Zen centers or meditation halls.

INDEX